LOVE
FULL
CIRCLE

Foundations
OF THE Faith

The Golden Rule

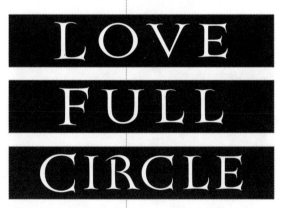

LOVE
FULL
CIRCLE

Doug McIntosh

MOODY PRESS
CHICAGO

ISBN: 0-8024-6647-8

1 3 5 7 9 10 8 6 4 2

Printed in the United States of America

To Cheryl, my dear wife,
a living demonstration of the power
and beauty of the Golden Rule

CONTENTS

ACKNOWLEDGMENTS

*A*ny book is the product of many lives, and this one is no exception. At the top of my thank-you list is Jim Bell of Moody Press, who offered me the opportunity to contribute this volume to the Foundations of the Faith series. Jim also wrote the helpful Review and Study Guide that concludes this book.

My appreciation is due also to longtime friend and colleague Tim Crater, who read portions of the manuscript and provided useful insights, and to Karen Bouchard, Cathy Daniell, and Emmie Loften, who read it in its entirety and offered a variety of important suggestions for improvement.

Special thanks go to Karen Hutto, whose keen editorial eye assisted my efforts in ways too numerous to mention, and to Kathy Berkstresser and Kay Himmel, staff members and friends whose cheerful service to the folks at Stone Mountain Community Church make my life so much easier.

Thanks also go to Jim Vincent of the Moody Press editorial staff for his many helpful ideas and suggestions.

Introduction

SIMPLE

GIFTS

Several years ago, someone told me a story about a woman who was on a panel of prospective jurors in a court case. When the defense attorney approached and asked her a question about serving on the jury, she balked. "I can't serve on this jury. I don't believe in capital punishment."

At that point the judge interjected, "You don't understand, madam. This is not a death penalty case. This is a civil trial. The defendant in this action is accused of taking his wife's money and spending it on gambling and other women."

The juror replied, "In that case, your honor, I'll be happy to serve, and I've changed my mind about capital punishment."

Modern man has a way of changing his mind frequently about matters of ethics—to the extent that he has any. For two generations in the United States, universities have taught that morals are humanly originated opinions, imposed by those in power to simplify the work of governing the populace. We are now reaping the fruit of that questionable point of view as those trained in the university systems reach positions of high authority.

A case in point is the recent furor over morals in the White House. Many of President Clinton's defenders acknowledge that the president lied under oath. However, they not only excused such lying; they insisted that lying in this instance was and is morally superior to telling the truth and having one's sexual misconduct exposed as a result. If that happens, these moral advisers contended, others in the witness's families could be humiliated and hurt, and that would be tragic. Little mention was made of the hurts of those voters who thought they were electing a man of integrity.

Marianne Jennings, a professor at Arizona State University, teaches legal and ethical studies. She says that her students seem to think that people who express moral principles are engaging in a form of "hate speech." The students believe that advocating moral principles is to show disregard, even hatred, to those who oppose such principles. To counter such faulty thinking, Jennings points to the ethical principles that have been recognized in cultures across the globe for centuries:

> One such standard of universal morality is what is referred to by Christians as the "Golden Rule": Do unto others as you would have them do unto you. The same notion of fairness can be found in the basic tenets of Buddhism, Judaism, Hinduism, and even in philosophy in the form of Kant's "categorical imperative." Throughout time, this simple test of ethics has been recognized in various

cultures as a means of preserving civility, decency, and morality. Its beauty lies in its simplicity.[1]

Indeed, the Golden Rule is divine shorthand. First expressed by Jesus in Matthew 7:12 (and repeated in Luke 6:31), the principles of behavior cut through secondary matters and focus on the core of what Jesus wants us to be and do. By sharing the Golden Rule's cogent summary of heavenly intent, the Lord Jesus reduced the goal of all our relationships to a single easily remembered command: Treat others the right way—the way you would have them treat you.

Here is a fundamental of the faith as basic as the Lord's Prayer and the Beatitudes. Each implies personal benefits; and in each Jesus demonstrates the mark of mastery in His simplification of a profound topic: praying, living a godly life, and showing a consistent, giving love.

Anybody can make things complicated, and some people appear to enjoy doing so, even preachers. I remember hearing the story of one distinguished Scottish preacher who was the guest speaker in a highland kirk. The visiting dignitary began the service with an erudite and lengthy pastoral prayer filled with four-syllable words. In the middle of this elevated conversation with the Almighty, the preacher felt a tug at his coattails. Annoyed, he turned around to discover the source of the interruption—an elderly lady, seated behind him in the choir loft. Whispering, she advised him, "Jes' call Him Fether, and ask 'im fer somethin'."

It takes skill and insight to summarize. A newspaperman, visiting the Oakland Raiders' football camp during the 1970s, had just come from the Jack London Historic

Monument. On a whim, he decided to read a portion of the author's prose to the Raiders' All-Pro quarterback, Ken Stabler. He chose London's passionate statement of personal mission: "I would rather be ashes than dust! I would rather that my spark should burn out in a brilliant blaze than it should be stifled by dry rot. I would rather be a superb meteor, every atom of me in magnificent glow, than a sleepy and permanent planet. The proper function of man is to live, not to exist. I shall not waste my days in trying to prolong them. I shall use my time." After reading this to the quarterback, the writer asked, "What does that mean to you?"

Stabler said, "Throw deep."[2]

The Golden Rule is the ethical equivalent of throwing deep. It is the way to make your life meaningful and use your time productively for God, yourself, and others. Especially because the Rule comes from the Lord Jesus (who formed a living exhibition of how it is to be done), every Christian ought to be an expert at loving people. We ought to know exactly what the Golden Rule means and how to apply it. We need to understand the likely obstacles that we will encounter in our efforts to love others as ourselves, and how to overcome them. We need to comprehend how we can make a difference in ourselves and in others by our obedience. We also need to appreciate the divine resources available to assist us as we carry out our ministry of loving people.

All of that is what this book is about.

NOTES

1. Marianne M. Jennings, "The Real Generation Gap," *Imprimis*, August 1998, 6.
2. James S. Hewett, ed., "Life and Risk," *Parables, Etc.*, November 1984, 1.

Chapter One

WHAT'S SO GOLDEN ABOUT THE GOLDEN RULE?

*A*nglican priest John Papworth made the news not long ago with his novel interpretation of a famous biblical text: "Jesus said love your neighbor. He didn't say love Marks & Spencers." By that terse remark, the ecclesiastic encouraged his parishioners to engage in the practice of selective shoplifting—for a good cause, naturally. Marks & Spencers is one of the largest chain stores in England. Papworth approved of stealing from large stores because they allegedly push smaller ones into economic distress, creating unemployment and poverty. "You can only steal from a person," he explained. "You can only have a moral relationship with a person." Corporate entities don't qualify.

Papworth had compartmentalized behavior, making it acceptable to steal under certain conditions, while it remained unacceptable under other conditions. The priest said about his church-sanctioned shoplifting, "I don't regard it as stealing. I regard it as a badly needed reallocation of economic resources."[1]

"A badly needed reallocation of economic resources" —words to live by for some people, yet I expect that most English Christians would reject the rector's morality, recognizing it as political propaganda masquerading as Christian ethics. Furthermore, some of those believers he addressed probably hold Marks & Spencers stock, and for them corporate losses from widespread theft would in time prove intensely personal.

Papworth's remarks, however, do illustrate how easy it is to lose one's grip on the most fundamental biblical teaching. Shoplifting certainly violates the Golden Rule, since people do not like having their things stolen, and in the end it is people who suffer. As big as Marks & Spencers may be, stealing goods from a department store injures the welfare of employees, managers, investors, and even customers (who ultimately pay higher prices to cover the losses). For Christians, nothing is more fundamental to the faith than Jesus' dictum, "Love your neighbor as yourself" (Matthew 22:39). This, the so-called Golden Rule, appears in several forms throughout the Scriptures. The version in Matthew 7:12 forms the punch line of what is known as the Sermon on the Mount (Matthew 5–7): "Whatever you want men to do to you, do also to them." Jesus often stated the Rule as the summary of how Christians are supposed to relate to others. It also formed, at a critical time, part of His answer to a loaded question.

SECOND PLACE IS PURE GOLD

"Of all the commandments, which is the most important?" (Mark 12:28 NIV). The scribe looked at

Jesus, waiting for an answer, while an uneasy hush fell over the crowd. It was an impossible inquiry as well as a dangerous one. The rabbis taught that there were 613 commands—365 negative ones and 248 positive ones—in God's law. They also debated at length which of them should be regarded as the most important; so, no matter which commandment the Teacher picked, He would be inviting ridicule from those learned and hostile scholars who favored a different top commandment. The religious authorities in the crowd were waiting to pounce on almost anything He would say, and it was no accident that they were present for this ticklish query.

Everywhere He had gone that week, Jesus had been surrounded by people, most of them admirers. However, as He taught in the temple precincts, it was clear that His enemies were becoming active. Rumors were flying that they had issued a warrant for His arrest but were waiting for the proper moment, when He would be out of the public eye (see Matthew 26:5). Some among them decided that in the interim it would be wise to discredit Him before the crowds. This should be easy to do, they reasoned. Jesus was inviting public responses to His teaching on a daily basis by speaking in the temple environs, swollen with people because of the impending holiday.

However, their attempts were thwarted. Jesus deftly handled the best His antagonists could offer, often revealing in His answers astonishing insight. His responses uncovered as well the shallowness and jealousy that lay beneath their challenges. Finally, they decided to pin Him; He was asked to single out the greatest commandment of all, putting one clearly above all else and, in so doing, perhaps demoting the rest.

The Teacher's answer came without hesitation: "The first of all the commandments is: 'Hear, O Israel, the Lord our God, the Lord is one. And you shall love the Lord your God with all your heart, with all your soul, with all your mind, and with all your strength.' This is the first commandment. And the second, like it, is this: 'You shall love your neighbor as yourself.' There is no other commandment greater than these" (Mark 12:29–31).

The crowd—including His enemies—must have been stunned. The Teacher had put His finger on the central thrust of God's law and summarized it in two brief statements. Even His questioner, a member of a group that had come to oppose Him, had to recognize the profoundness of His response: "Well said, Teacher. You have spoken the truth, for there is one God, and there is no other but He. And to love Him with all the heart, with all the understanding, with all the soul, and with all the strength, and to love one's neighbor as oneself, is more than all the whole burnt offerings and sacrifices" (Mark 12:32–33). Following this startling summation of God's truth, Jesus' enemies abandoned new theological attacks: "After that no one dared question Him" (Mark 12:34).

Here, then, from the mouth of Jesus the Messiah, is Christian morality:

- Rule One: Love God supremely.
- Rule Two: Love your neighbor as yourself.
- Rules Three and Following: See Rules One and Two.

All morality, and every strategy to honor God's kingdom, spring from these first two rules.

Notice that Rule Two's importance issues from Rule One. Loving God totally leads to treasuring the things God treasures; and humanity, such as we are, is what He holds dear. This is why we are to love others. Augustine said long ago, "Love God supremely, and do what you want." Does that sound contradictory? It is a fully biblical sentiment, for loving God supremely will always lead us into loving others. We will want to please God, and we will please God by loving Him and others.

TO BECOME INDISPENSABLE

IGNORE OTHERS . . .

Today, however, there is a great deal of skepticism about the Golden Rule, or about almost any rule. Modern minds find moral absolutes uncomfortable and look for ways to dismiss them. For instance, one jaded contemporary expression of Jesus' words asserts that "Those who have the gold make the rules."

Another modern cynic has built a business around her version: "Treat others as they have treated you." For a fee of about fifty dollars, the operator of "Revenge Unlimited" will deliver a collection of party disfavors to your favorite enemy: wilted flowers wrapped in dirty newspaper, deflated balloons, melted chocolates, year-old conical hats, and the like. As an optional service, she also will present cheap champagne and write personalized "revenge-o-gram" poems (especially recommended for ex-spouses). "Nobody sells revenge," the proprietor explained. "There are people who deliver flowers for Mother's Day or Valentine's Day for love or romance or respect or acknowledgement; but we're after bad jokes and getting even."[2] American ingenuity strikes again.

Even some Christians wonder whether loving their neighbors can make much of a difference. After all, we live in a world moving toward personal isolation. Increasing numbers of people work at home via computers. Hungry consumers can order groceries and other necessities on the Internet and have them delivered to the door. Home entertainment centers and cable TV cause us to cocoon in the evenings, instead of visiting friends or even a nearby movie theater with our neighbors. Some of us live in condominiums or apartments where we come and go without getting to know anyone. Few chances exist for natural meetings over backyard fences, and busy work or home schedules can make time with others seem less important, even unrealistic. As a result, few people know their neighbors, much less exercise Christian love toward them.

... AND NEVER BE MISSED

Modern culture tends to make us little islands of self-sufficiency in a sea of indifference. Consider George Mason. George's life was wrapped up in his work. He lived by himself, and even during the holidays kept to himself, though he was invited to a few social gatherings. People weren't terrifically important in George's life.

One Christmas Eve, after his employees had gone home, George entered his office vault to pick up some extra cash for the holiday. To his dismay, the large vault door, with freshly oiled hinges, swung closed behind him. The lights went out as he heard the automatic locks click into place. Too late, he realized that no one could hear his panicky cries for help. And the next day was Christmas, so no one would be in the office!

For a while he was concerned about suffocation. Then he remembered the salesman referring to a "safety vent" in the vault for just such an occurrence. He managed to find it in the darkness and bring air into his confined quarters.

Christmas Eve and Christmas Day came and went. He was uncomfortable, hungry, thirsty, in pitch darkness —and profoundly alone.

The next morning, the company's chief cashier arrived and unlocked the vault, leaving the door ajar. Without anyone seeing him, Mason staggered out, blinking, and made it to the water cooler. He then took a taxi to his home and freshened up. Back at the office, it was obvious that nobody had missed him. The indifference of people made him think.

After his experience, George placed a card on the wall of the vault to remind him of what he had learned. It read, "To love people, to be indispensable somewhere, that is the purpose of life. That is the secret of happiness."[3] Many people have suffered more and learned less; but if George had taken the Golden Rule seriously, the lesson might have come sooner.

BECOME INDISPENSABLE BY BEING INVOLVED

To be indispensable somewhere requires being involved in people's lives. That's where the Golden Rule comes in. Those who practice it make their mark on people.

None of us at the church I serve will ever forget Barb Taylor's funeral. Barb's husband, Chuck, was (and is) a church staff member, and the Taylors were active members of the church long before he came onto the staff. Barb was a great practitioner of the Golden Rule. She was interested in everybody and had a wonderful way of communicating love to people. While I enjoyed dinner with the Taylors one evening, she confessed that she was struggling with a problem.

"What might that be?" I asked.

"Lots of people call me and tell me their troubles," she explained. "I don't really feel qualified to counsel them. And I don't tell them anything particularly profound, but they keep calling, and I think about their problems a lot. It sometimes keeps me awake at night."

The telephone calls, of course, were the product of her loving concern for others. They sensed that she was the genuine article. The love of Christ showed through even after she began to suffer from the cancer that finally took her life.

Her funeral was standing room only, filled to overflowing with people whose lives she had touched. At the end, I gave a gospel invitation, and at least two people that I know of trusted Christ that day. It wasn't, however, due to my preaching. I said very little. After a time of prayer and Scripture reading, we placed an open microphone at the front of the auditorium and invited people who wanted to say something in remembrance to step forward and do so. With five hundred people in the room and mankind's innate fear of public speaking, we had no idea what would happen.

It became the longest funeral I've ever attended, and one of the most joyful.

Fifteen to twenty people walked to the microphone.

All related examples of Barb's loving investment in them. Perhaps the most profound was eleven-year-old Kent Suter. His face streaming with tears, Kent stepped to the microphone and with great difficulty managed to say, "Mrs. Taylor loved me—a lot." He tried to say more, but couldn't get out the words. He simply cried for a few seconds and resumed his seat, but his message came through with great eloquence. So did hers.

The loving life is an eloquent life. Love people as yourself and your message will be clear and respected. You will become indispensable whether that is your aim or not. There are never enough lovers—in terms of those living out the pure love of the Golden Rule—to go around. Practicing the Rule is the infrequently tapped mother lode when it comes to making an impact on each generation.

THE GOLDEN RULE IN ACTION ... AND INACTION

A WORD ASSOCIATION

Unfortunately, the church's participation in demonstrating the Golden Rule isn't all that visible in the modern world. Ask ten non-Christians at random what pops into their heads when they hear the word "Christian" today. Chances are that a large number of responses won't be complimentary. You might hear words like *hypocritical, self-righteous, mercenary,* and even a number of unprintable adjectives.

Not all those criticisms will be valid, to be sure; but a great many of the complaints of people outside the faith come because no genuine Christian is involved in their lives. When they think of Christians, they think of televangelists, media caricatures, and talk show hosts, not the person next door. Christians may live near them, but those Christians have little contact.

A POWERFUL DEMONSTRATION

It was not always so. Consider, for example, the letter of Aristides to Hadrian, the Roman Emperor. Aristides, a second-century Greek philosopher, became a follower of Christ in his late fifties, after he was already widely known in the Roman Empire. Hadrian (A.D. 117–138) had sanctioned the persecution and killing of Christians. In A.D. 125, Aristides wrote the emperor in an appeal to have the persecution ended. The philosopher buttressed his arguments with an appeal to common Christian behavior and beliefs:

> They know God, the Creator and Fashioner of all things ... and beside Him they worship no other God. They have the commands of the Lord Jesus Christ Himself graven upon their hearts; and they observe them, looking forward to the resurrection of the dead and life in the world to come. They do not commit adultery nor fornication, nor bear false witness, nor covet the things of others; they honour father and mother, and love their neighbours; they judge justly, and they never do to others what they would not wish to happen to themselves; they appeal to those who injure them, and try to win them as friends; they are eager to do good to their enemies; they are gentle and easy to be entreated; they abstain from all unlawful conversation and from all impurity; they despise not the widow, nor oppress the orphan; and he that has, gives ungrudgingly for the maintenance of him who has not.
>
> If they see a stranger, they take him under their roof,

and rejoice over him as over a very brother; for they call themselves brethren not after the flesh but after the spirit....

And whenever one of their poor passes from the world, each one of them according to his ability gives heed to him and carefully sees to his burial. And if they hear that one of their number is imprisoned or afflicted on account of the name of their Messiah, all of them anxiously minister to his necessity, and if it is possible to redeem him they set him free. And if there is among them any that is poor and needy, and if they have no spare food, they fast two or three days in order to supply to the needy their lack of food. They observe the precepts of their Messiah with much care, living justly and soberly as the Lord their God commanded them.[4]

That a well-known philosopher could write such commendations at a time when Christianity was still an illegal religion explains a lot. Among other things, it gives the overriding reason why the faith expanded so rapidly in its first century in spite of official persecution. The early church exemplified its Lord by its behavior in conforming to the Golden Rule. Love consistently expressed is a hard thing to resist.

Throughout history, when believers have put the Rule into operation, human experience has been sweetened. Many of the blessings that we take for granted today as part of Western civilization issued from committed Christians who cared enough to give their prayers, their money, and their labors for the betterment of mankind. Child labor laws, the repeal of slavery, the six-day work week, the Red Cross, the Salvation Army, most of the charitable medical work that goes on around the world, the elevation of women, rescue missions all over the Western world, democratic institutions, and dozens of other blessings all emerged from Christians who sought to love their neighbors as themselves.

THE UNIVERSAL MINISTRY: ENCOURAGEMENT

And then there is that ministry of the Golden Rule that can be the most powerful of all—the practice of encouragement. Not everybody can establish an international relief agency or write legislation curbing slavery, but encouragement is a kindness within the reach of every believer. And what a glory it is to both giver and recipient!

A Methodist minister of a past generation, William Stidger of Boston, once fell into a terrible depression. During this time, a wise friend advised him to deal with the problem by reaching out to others with encouragement and thanksgiving. Stidger sat down and began to recall the benefits he had received from other people. An English teacher soon came to mind. He had studied under her years before, and she had instilled in him a love of poetry that stayed with him all his life. He pulled out some stationery and penned a letter of thanks to the woman, who by this time was well advanced in years.

The letter he received in reply began: "My dear Willie." That helped him right away. By this time he was stout and bald, a respected scholar, and he doubted that there was anybody left in the world who would call him "Willie." She wrote: "My dear Willie, I cannot tell you how much your note meant to me. I am in my eighties, living alone in a small room, cooking my own meals, lonely and, like the last leaf of autumn, lingering behind. You will be interested to know that I taught school for fifty years and yours is the first note of appreciation I ever received. It came on a blue-cold morning and it cheered me as nothing has in many years."

A nearly tangible brightness entered William Stidger's heart as he read those words. It evaporated part of the fog of his spiritual lethargy, and he began to write words of encouragement to other people. During the process, his interest in ministry was renewed and invigorated because he took that first step of encouraging another.[5]

Then there is the episode of James Anderson Burns. He was quite different from William Stidger: more self-reliant, more independent. Yet his life, too, turned a corner when a gesture of encouragement came his way at a strategic moment. Burns's story took place in the tiny community in the eastern Kentucky mountains where I was born. Oneida was even tinier right before the end of the nineteenth century, and almost inaccessible from the outside world. The only road into town was the creek. If it was low, you steered your wagon into it and drove upstream to town. If it was in flood, you had to wait, or leave your wagon and walk the trails.

The unforgiving terrain and inadequate transportation conspired to produce great poverty in the area. Children grew up with few educational opportunities.

Not only was Oneida isolated and poor, it was dangerous. Since the Civil War, a feud between two prominent families had torn the community. Every few months an outburst of revenge-motivated violence would take place.

On a fateful day in the 1890s, Burns, a Baptist preacher, hiked into Oneida, met the leaders of the warring families, and made them a proposition: If they would lay down their arms, he would build a school to educate their children. For once, the prospect of a better life for their children overcame the villagers' antagonisms. They agreed.

Burns traveled all over the eastern United States afterward, sharing his vision and raising funds to buy materials. The work was excruciatingly difficult, slow, and subject to many setbacks. Though he was a powerful man with great gifts, at one point James Burns became greatly discouraged. With the initial building still unfinished, the construction materials (brought in at great effort) exhausted, and the bank account empty, he hit bottom. Kneeling at the site in tears, he prayed, "Lord, if You want this school to come into existence, You're going to have to show me You're still in it. I don't have any strength left."

When Burns stood up, he saw a wagon headed toward him, pulled by two mules and driven by a local farmer. It contained a load of used lumber for the construction of the school. Lacking money himself, *the farmer had torn the ceilings out of his house* and brought the lumber so that the building could be finished.[6]

It was just the encouragement Burns needed, and from that point he never looked back. Oneida Baptist Institute was born, grew rapidly, and since has educated hundreds of mountain children, including my own parents. The school has produced pastors, educators, doctors, missionaries, successful entrepreneurs, and even a governor of Kentucky. Sometimes encouragement is worth much more than money, and all that is necessary to produce it is one person with an obedient heart.

Or, if you prefer, don't regard it as obedience. Just think of it as a badly needed reallocation of spiritual resources.

NOTES

1. "The Papworth Principle," *World,* 29 March 1997, 7.
2. I found Revenge Unlimited on the Internet, along with the owner's unusual mission statement. The Internet address is www.revengeunlimited.com.
3. Told by George Bogan, "Christmas," *Wilde's Illustration Service,* November 1983, 36.
4. "The Apology of Aristides the Philosopher," translated from the Greek and from the Syriac version in parallel columns by D. M. Kay. From the Internet at www.newadvent.org/fathers/1012.htm.
5. William Stidger, *More Sermons in Stories* (New York: Abingdon Cokesbury, 1954), 117–18.
6. The story of the Institute's founding is beautifully chronicled in the photographic essay *Dawn Comes to the Mountains,* ed. Samuel W. Thomas (Louisville, Ky.: George Rogers Clark Press, 1981).

Chapter Two

WHY DOES IT HAVE TO BE A RULE?

*C*huck Colson, president of Prison Fellowship and an evangelical author, told a story at a Washington conference several years ago that I have never forgotten. He described how, during the 1950s, three of America's most accomplished speakers set out on a preaching tour. Donald Grey Barnhouse, Harold John Ockenga, and Marcellus Kik traveled by train around the country, speaking in churches in a series of cities over a period of thirty days. All three preachers commanded a national following, and large crowds attended each meeting.

Since the tour was so strenuous, only two of the three would speak in a given service, giving the other the evening off. After a challenging month, they came at last to the final stop on the tour, a Presbyterian church in Richmond, Virginia.

Ockenga was scheduled to speak first, followed by Barnhouse. Although Ockenga and Kik had varied the sermons they used as the tour progressed, Barnhouse had given the same sermon every time. By this time Ockenga had heard Barnhouse's regular sermon some twenty times, and as the hour of the final meeting approached, a mischievous idea began to form in his brilliant and retentive mind. Later he stepped to the lectern and delivered Barnhouse's stock sermon, virtually word for word. As he was speaking, he glanced behind him from time to time to see how Dr. Barnhouse was taking all this. (Anyone who speaks in public settings can appreciate the terror that the situation might provoke in the victim.) Barnhouse, however, appeared stoic and impassive.

Ockenga finished and sat down, trying in vain to resist the smile that kept forming on his face. Barnhouse then arose and flawlessly gave a completely different sermon. When the evening ended and the two preachers had left the church together, Barnhouse still had said nothing about what Ockenga had done. Finally, with tongue firmly planted in cheek, Ockenga referred to his prank, saying, "Donald, they liked your sermon tonight."

Barnhouse replied, "Yes, but not as much as they did when I gave it here three months ago."

Invalid assumptions can cause pain and embarrassment. Like Dr. Ockenga's practical joke, what we don't know can spring up and bite us when we least expect it. In the same way, a lot of people assume they understand what love is when in reality they don't, and the effects can be catastrophic.

In Western culture, most people think love is fundamentally emotional in character. Our sentiments must be stirred deeply, or we haven't loved—or so goes the popular concept. Since everyone possesses a finite amount of emotional capital, the idea of being obliged to love the entire human race tires people out just thinking about it. As a result, many Christians secretly consider the Golden Rule a nice idea, but impossible to obey in real life.

Far from being simply a pleasant ideal, however, God made the Golden Rule the lifeblood of healthy human experience. Obey it, and life becomes richer for the one who loves and the one who is loved. Ignore it, and the world becomes a dark and forbidding place.

LOVE HAPPENS?

Biblical love differs profoundly from the cultural concept of love that so dominates Western thinking (and which has influenced the church so profoundly). The fundamental difference between biblical love and the romantic love portrayed in art, literature, and films can be seen most clearly in the direction of each. Romantic love happens to me. It is love in the passive voice. It crushes and overwhelms (in a pleasing way). I "fall in love." But its power is also its weakness: Since I have no control over it, it can leave just as suddenly as it comes. In contrast, biblical love is active; it's a choice we can make.

Modern culture likes the idea that attraction to another person can be so grand and all-encompassing that it bypasses the reason. Romantic love is mindless yet emotion filled. One can't help the feeling. If you read romantic fiction, somewhere you have seen a description like this: "Their eyes met across the dance floor. Though the room was filled with people, they saw no one but each other. The orchestra began to play, matching the symphony in their hearts. He approached and extended his strong arms. Without a word, she glided into them."

And the rest, as they say, is history.

What they don't say, however, is that the irrationality of modern romance often leaves a trail of blood and pain in its wake. Novels and films rarely refer to the abandoned wife, left behind to raise a family alone, or to the suicides, or to the children who suffer from dreadful insecurities, or to the alienated friends. Romance has little time for such things; it pursues an agenda that sees only the object of its desire. In one popular movie of a few years ago, the hero, a modern sophisticate, trains a timid young man how to talk to the girl of his dreams: "Tell her she is everything to you, that she is your destiny." Mr. Milquetoast, however, misreads his notes at the moment of truth, and tells her instead, "You are my density." How true, how true.

Before you accuse me of lacking romance, remember that as a pastor I have a peculiar slant on this matter. I have had to deal with too many "victims" of the departure of romantic love. By "victim" I mean not the wounded mate but the adulterer.

When talking with people who have left their mates for someone new, I typically will hear the offender justify his or her treachery by referring to the power of romance: "I didn't plan it this way; my attraction to her (him) just happened. It just proves I didn't love my wife (husband) to begin with." In the twisted logic of illicit affection, it is considered dishonest (and thus immoral) to resist a deeply felt new attraction. Even the past must be revised to accommodate the new ultimate "reality." But expecting emotions to take the lead tends to create passiveness and ready-made excuses for not taking a proactive interest in the lives of others.

LOVE IN THE ACTIVE VOICE

By contrast to the romantic love of pop culture, biblical love is in the active voice. Biblical love is founded on choices. It never leaves because it is always within my capacities. There are no victims to biblically applied love, only beneficiaries.

Instead of being mindless, biblical love is intelligent. Those who engage it know what they're getting into—lots of challenges and difficulties—and they practice it anyway, because they know that it pleases God. After all, it imitates His own heart. The central expression of biblical love is found in John 3:16, which says, "For God so loved the world that He gave His only begotten Son, that whoever believes in Him should not perish but have everlasting life." God did not give His Son because our beauty and goodness compelled Him to act. He made the choice with all its painful ramifications, and at the crucial moment did not shrink from doing what was best for us.

Biblical love's essence is joyfully choosing to take action to promote the welfare of another. God loved us and chose to take action to promote our well-being. He gave His Son—precisely the One we needed to solve our problems of alienation from Him and each other. The loving is in the giving. God loved greatly, so He gave lavishly. And that's why we have the Rule—to follow God and model His love to a world seeking real love.

THE THREE LOVES

This definition of love as choices leading to action may be seen as radical, but it is common to the vocabulary of the New Testament, which describes three types of love. In the common Greek of the time, each word contributed a different spice to God's love recipe. Though there is some overlap in their definitions, each word possesses its own flavor. Here's a summary of each:

1. *Philia.* This is *the love of attraction*—the attraction that comes from seeing worth in the object loved. For example, "The Father loves [*phileo,* the verb form] the Son, and shows Him all things that He Himself does" (John 5:20). Likewise, Jesus told the disciples, "The Father Himself loves [*phileo*] you, because you have loved [*phileo*] Me, and have believed that I came forth from God" (John 16:27). The disciples were attracted by the worth of the Son. The Father, in turn, saw their worth in their relationship to His Son.

   Philia, by the way, is not "inferior" to *agape,* the characteristic word for Christian love; it has its place in the divine scheme of things. Indeed, valid romantic love possesses a healthy dose of *philia,* or at least it should. (There also should be an unalterable measure of *agape* to back it up when the beloved behaves unattractively.)

2. *Storge* (pronounced *store-gay*) is *the love of natural affection,* notably love for children, parents, and other close relatives. It is significant only when it is missing. Indeed, that is how it takes its place in the New Testament—in descriptions where its absence constitutes a mark of degeneracy. For example, the Apostle Paul says that men apart from God are "backbiters, haters of God . . . unloving [*astorgos*[1]]" (Romans 1:30–31). *Storge* is never commanded in Scripture. It is expected to be there in response to the investment of caring parents and siblings.

3. The most common word for love in the New Testament is *agape*; this is *the love of determination.* It overcomes obstacles and even unattractiveness in the person

loved to do good for that person. Its driving force is the character of God: "We love Him, because He first loved us" (1 John 4:19). *Agape* is love that can be commanded, because it depends on the will. One writer calls it "unconquerable benevolence."[2]

One more thing about *agape,* the only love that the Bible commands Christians to demonstrate: *Agape* was a new idea that appeared almost exclusively in the New Testament with the coming of Christ. Theologian and author J. I. Packer said:

> The Greek word *agape* (love) seems to have been virtually a Christian invention—a new word for a new thing (apart from about twenty occurrences in the Greek version of the Old Testament, it is almost non-existent before the New Testament). *Agape* draws its meaning directly from the revelation of God in Christ. It is not a form of natural affection, however intense, but a supernatural fruit of the Spirit (Gal. 5:22). It is a matter of will rather than feeling (for Christians must love even those they dislike . . .). It is the basic element in Christlikeness.[3]

While *agape* might be a new term, the concept is as old as time. It was God's eternal *agape* that compelled Christ to go to the Cross. *Agape* is also the word that appears in the texts containing the Golden Rule: "You shall love *[agapao]* your neighbor as yourself" (Mark 12:31). And it is the term so beautifully pictured in the classic Pauline description of love in 1 Corinthians 13:4–8.

SIXTEEN GEMS IN THE CROWN

First Corinthians 13:4–8 describes sixteen marks of biblical love. It would be wrong to say that a person is loveless if he falls short of some of these qualities. Rather, these words describe love in full maturity—the ultimate goal of the Golden Rule. These sixteen gems reflect the glory of Christ in our lives. The more they sparkle in our lives, the more Christ receives honor in our attitudes and actions.

FIVE GEMS FROM VERSE FOUR

Verse four contains five gems of biblical love. First, "love *suffers long*" (13:4, all italics added). The Greek word underlying "suffers long" suggests the ability to wait on people to change for the better. One church father, Chrysostom, insisted that patience of this sort issues from strength; it comes from a person who has the ability to take his own revenge but refuses to do so.[4] Instead of indicating weakness, it displays uncommon fortitude.

Abraham Lincoln exhibited long-suffering in his dealings with Edwin Stanton, his secretary of war. Stanton once called Lincoln "the original gorilla" and wondered aloud why anyone would travel to Africa looking for those animals when such a prime specimen could be found in Springfield, Illinois. Despite receiving such sarcastic remarks, Lincoln later appointed Stanton over the War Department on his merits. The president returned only kindness to Stanton. When Lincoln breathed his last after being shot at Ford's Theater, it was Stanton who tearfully said, "There lies the greatest ruler of men the world has ever seen."[5] Love's long-suffering had at last won him over.

Second, "love ... *is kind*" (verse 4). It is unsatisfied with simply waiting; it looks for ways to help or benefit others. Instead of wondering what the new neighbors are like, it bakes a peach cobbler and takes it over to welcome them.

Third, "love *does not envy*" (verse 4). The Greek word Paul used in this expression does double duty in New Testament Greek. It can mean either *to be jealous* or *to be envious*. With jealousy, we want what another has; with envy, we wish the other person didn't have it. Biblical love is glad when another person prospers. It can sincerely rejoice at the other's success.

Fourth, "love *does not parade itself*" (13:4). People who love others do not call attention to what they are doing for them. They are content to make their choices and actions quietly and to express them in ways that benefit those they love. They are not motivated by what the objects of their kindness can do for them in return. They also refuse to be condescending to the people they love.

The final gem found in verse 4 reads: "Love . . . *is not puffed up*." That is, love is not inflated by grandiose notions of its own importance. It is concerned with the good of the person being loved, not the importance or recognition of the one doing the loving. William Carey, the father of the modern missionary movement, went to India at great cost to himself. He eventually translated the Bible into dozens of Indian dialects, but when he first arrived there some of the British residents regarded him with disdain. At one gathering of stuffed shirts, someone said to him in a loud voice, "I hear, Mr. Carey, that you once worked as a shoemaker."

"No, your lordship," Carey responded, "not a shoemaker, only a cobbler."[6] He refused to take credit even for making shoes, only for mending them. He was not in India to impress the expatriates; he went there to bring the Word of God to the people.

WHAT LOVE DOES NOT DO

Eleven other gems can be mined in verses 5–8 of 1 Corinthians 13. Each shows another facet of this marvelous agape love. Let's look at each.

"Love . . . *does not behave rudely*" (verse 5). Tact and winsome behavior are the twin escorts of biblical love. Loving your neighbor requires respecting him first, and that means not throwing up barriers to God's purposes by the way you act. One writer observed, "Some of us are altogether too much inclined to claim for this truth which is God's the hearing it deserves; and always it gets only the hearing we can win for it."[7] Those who behave gracelessly lose that crucial forum.

"Love . . . *does not seek its own*" (verse 5). Love forms the antidote to the poisonous self-obsessions of Western culture. Those who love do not seek self-fulfillment, self-justification, or self-worth at the expense of another. Love looks to benefit its object, not the giver.

"Love . . . *is not provoked*" (verse 5). Mature biblical love refuses to be exasperated with people. Failure to bridle one's temper can produce one moment of madness which can undo a prolonged period of investment in others. Genuine love begins with recognition that its ministries often go unappreciated and a determination to do good whether credit is given or not.

"Love . . . *does not take into account a wrong suffered*" (verse 5 NASB). Paul's use of an accounting term in this expression teaches that love does not keep a record of wrongs suffered. People who obey the Golden Rule choose to not lay plans for future revenge. They know revenge is incompatible with *agape*.

During the Korean War, a South Korean Christian civilian was arrested and ordered shot by communist insurgents. However, a zealous young communist leader, hearing that the Christian operated an orphanage, decided to impose a more sadistic treatment. He ordered that the man's son be executed instead. The nineteen-year-old was brought forward and shot in the father's presence.

Later, when the tide of war had changed and the communist army had lost control of the area, the young communist leader was captured by U. N. forces and condemned to death for his war crimes. However, the Christian whose son had been executed interceded for the killer. "Give him to me," he said, "and I will train him." His request was granted, and he took his son's murderer into his own home. Eventually the man became a Christian pastor in South Korea.[8]

"Love . . . *does not rejoice in iniquity*" (verse 6). Obedience to the Golden Rule implies a more appropriate reaction would be grief, followed by prayer for the fallen person and (where possible) caring actions to promote his healing. Still less should Christians rejoice at the moral downfall of a rival; indeed, we should not regard others as rivals to begin with. Consequently we ought to refuse to make the phone call to a friend to share damaging information "that we might pray more intelligently."

WHAT LOVE DOES

"Love . . . *rejoices in the truth*" (verse 6). Loving others means taking pleasure in the victories of the gospel. Such victories take the form of kindnesses extended, forgiveness granted, and hearts changed through conversion and faith in Christ.

"Love . . . *bears all things*" (verse 7). The apostle recognized that love too often finds barriers in the foibles of people who are its objects. Those obstacles will not deter it, however. One translation has it, "There is nothing love cannot face."[9] Biblical love is not blind; it merely sees beyond the present challenges to the victories ahead.

When Simon Peter was brought to Jesus the first time, the Lord said to him, "'You are Simon the son of Jonah. You shall be called Cephas' (which is translated, A Stone)" (John 1:42). Jesus' new disciple was by nature and name a Simon ("vacillator"), but in time he would become a rock. The Lord Jesus must have found Peter taxing at times, but His love bore those weaknesses for the sake of the man Peter became.

"Love . . . *believes all things*" (verse 7). Love chooses to believe the best about a person. People all over the world are looking for someone to believe in them. When they find such a person, it can be transforming.

One of my favorite seminary professors, Howard Hendricks, is known today as one of the world's most capable teachers. Based on his history as he shared it in class, however, you would never have predicted an academic career for him when he was younger. Dr. Hendricks says he can remember only two of his childhood schoolteachers: those of his fifth and sixth grade years. He had gained, by the fifth grade, a reputation for causing trouble in the classroom. His fifth grade teacher dealt with Howie by tying him to his seat and wrapping mucilage paper over his mouth.

For several obscure reasons, Dr. Hendricks reports, he was promoted to the sixth grade, where his new teacher immediately impressed him. For one thing, she was 6 feet-4 inches tall and, to quote him, was "sort of a feminine version of Sherlock Holmes." As he walked into her class the first day, she said, "Oh, you're Howard Hendricks. I've heard a lot about you."

Then she stunned him by adding, "But I don't believe a word of it!"

She convinced him, instead, that she believed in *him*. As a result, young Howie knocked himself out to please her. Word got out during that school year about the change in his approach to academic things, and every few days Howie would look up and see the face of his fifth grade teacher framed in the little glass window in the door. She could hardly believe it was Howie, but all he needed was someone to believe in him.

"Love . . . *hopes all things*" (verse 7). Another way to put this is, "Love refuses to give up on people." Back before the 1972 Billy Graham Crusade in Atlanta, I attended a series of meetings led by Charlie Riggs. Charlie's love of people and vast knowledge about ministry in a crusade setting impressed me.

Charlie came to Christ as a young man and was nurtured in the faith by Lorne Sanny, who in turn was being discipled by Navigators' founder Dawson Trotman. Charlie was a bit rough around the edges and, to Lorne, seemed to showed little promise as a Christian leader. Charlie's slow development so disheartened his mentor that Lorne once complained to Dawson about it. Trotman wrote back and said, "Stay with your man. You never know what God will do with him."

So, Lorne Sanny continued to work with Charlie Riggs, who in time became a member of the staff of the Navigators. In 1952, the Navigators loaned Charlie to the

Billy Graham team to handle follow-up in their crusades. Though Charlie planned to return to the Navigators eventually, he worked out so well that he stayed with Billy Graham. In 1957, on the eve of the famous New York City Crusade at Madison Square Garden, the crusade director suddenly had to be replaced. Whom could they get? The lay chairman suggested Charlie Riggs, but Billy Graham wasn't sure if Charlie could handle the challenge.

The layman insisted; Charlie Riggs got the job and did it extremely well. The New York campaign became a model for the many crusades that would follow. Lorne Sanny didn't give up on Charlie, and it paid dividends.[10]

The one who loves biblically is no Pollyanna; he recognizes the waywardness of the heart. However, he also recognizes God's power to change that same heart. Love's hope is anchored ultimately in God, not in a rose-tinted view of the innate virtue of others.

"Love . . . *endures all things*" (13:7). Love's endurance is never passive. When obstacles arise, the biblical lover accepts them in stride, recognizing that hurdling them is simply part of the process of loving people. He or she still loves the person. Difficulties may be painful, but overcoming them will impress the person you love that your love is genuine. There is no substitute for hearing someone say, "We've been through a lot together, haven't we?"

"Love *never fails*" (verse 8). Paul's expression here is ambiguous, perhaps intentionally so. He may have been saying that love never fails to achieve its divinely intended goals, or that a person who determines to love others will always find a way to do so. Either idea is true. The Golden Rule produces results, and those who want to live it can always find a way to make love happen.

CLINICAL LOVE?

Hearing that the love required by the Golden Rule begins in the realm of the will, some objectors ask: Is Christian love supposed to be emotionless? Are Christians supposed to be detached people, merely concentrating on actions and indifferent to the people those actions benefit?

Of course not. Even if you attempted to become a person like that, you wouldn't be able to. Love shapes the giver as much as (or more than) the recipients. Over time, emotions will develop to accompany willful acts of love. (I will have much more to say on this in chapter 5, "The Golden Paradox.")

The reason for the emphasis on the will in the biblical vocabulary is to anticipate the convenient excuse that we enjoy giving ourselves—that loving others is beyond our control. It isn't. You and I can love people if we choose to do so. Obedience to the Golden Rule does not require heroic effort. As Samuel Johnson once said, "Kindness is in our power, even when fondness is not."[11] Nor do we need to be neglectful of our own welfare in order to obey it.

FOR OUR GOOD

All God's rules are given, in fact, to make us better people. God's command to love others as ourselves is given as much to enlarge our souls as to fulfill His purposes in the world.

When Jesus answered the scribe's question ("Which is the first commandment of all?") in Mark 12:28, He quoted Scripture, including Deuteronomy 10:12. The latter passage, given by Moses to Israel as they waited to enter the Promised Land, contains an enlightening post-script. Moses asked the people, "What does the Lord your God require of you, but to fear the Lord your God, to walk in all His ways and to love Him, to serve the Lord your God with all your heart and with all your soul, and to keep the commandments of the Lord and His statutes which I command you today *for your good?*" (Deuteronomy 10:12–13, italics added).

The importance of these final words can hardly be overstated. The chances are excellent that we will never be as devoted to God and His Word as we should be unless we understand that its precepts were given to make our lives better. Obedience to the Golden Rule sprouts from a firm belief that God's rules are themselves born from His love: "For this is the love of God, that we keep His commandments. And His commandments are not burdensome" (1 John 5:3). Indeed, they illuminate the gentle path to spiritual health for others and for ourselves.

NOTES

1. The Greek letter *alpha* (A) in the word indicates the negative of what follows.
2. William Barclay, *The Letters to the Galatians and Ephesians* (Philadelphia: Westminster, 1976), 50.
3. James I. Packer, *Your Father Loves You* (Wheaton, Ill.: Harold Shaw, 1986), 33.
4. John Chrysostom, "Homily on the First Epistle of St. Paul the Apostle," in *The AGES Digital Library Collections: The Nicene and Post-Nicene Fathers,* first series, vol. 12, ed. Philip Schaff. CD-ROM; Macintosh version 6 (Albany, Ore.: AGES Software, 1998), 438.
5. William Barclay, *The Letters to the Corinthians* (Philadelphia: Westminster, 1975), 120.
6. Ibid., 121.

7. Paul Scherer, quoted in Sue Nichols, *Words on Target* (Richmond, Va.: John Knox, 1963), 5.

8. As told in J. Allen Blair, *First Corinthians: Devotional Studies on Living Wisely* (Neptune, N.J.: Loizeaux, 1969), 271.

9. *The New English Bible* (Oxford Univ., 1970).

10. Ray Pritchard, "Get in Over Your Head," *On the Father Front,* vol. 8, no. 2, Summer 1995; as quoted [online] at the Biblical Studies Foundation web site: www.bible.org/illus/c/c-19.htm.

11. Quoted in Jack Canfield, Mark Victor Hansen, Patty Aubery, and Nancy Mitchell, *Chicken Soup for the Christian Soul* (Deerfield Beach, Fla: Health Communications, 1997), 300.

Chapter Three

WHO IS MY NEIGHBOR?

A classic story about an army private during the Vietnam era describes how the soldier began to exhibit some unusual behavior shortly after reaching his assignment. As he walked about the camp each day, the private would pick up stray pieces of paper lying on the ground, examine each closely for a few seconds, and then discard it, saying to himself in a disappointed voice, "That's not it!"

This went on for about six months, at which time his bizarre behavior was brought to the attention of his superiors. They ordered him to report to the base psychiatrist, who came directly to the point when he asked: "What is wrong with you? What is your problem?"

With a baffled expression on his face, the soldier asked, "What problem? I don't have a problem."

The psychiatrist said, "There must be something wrong with you. I have heard that you wander around this base picking up pieces of paper and saying, 'That's

not it; that's not it!' Tell me—just what is it you are looking for?"

The man shook his head slowly and said, "I don't
know. I just don't seem to be able to find it."

The psychiatrist dismissed the man and went into
consultation with some of his colleagues. After reaching
a diagnosis, they called in the soldier and told him, "We
think your problem is serious, and we're going to give
you a medical discharge from the service."

When the psychiatrist handed the discharge paper to
him, the soldier took one look at it, leaped to his feet, and
shouted, "This is it! This is it!"

When it comes to loving their neighbors as themselves, a lot of people take an approach similar to that soldier's in deciding which people fall within the scope of
the word "neighbor." In short, they seem to be seeking
official authorization to escape their obligations.

DISCOVERING MY NEIGHBOR

A case in point is the scribe who decided to put the
Lord Jesus to the test publicly one day (a dangerous practice, as he discovered). The subject was eternal life and
how to have it. The Lord turned the tables on the scholar
and asked him, "What is written in the law? What is your
reading of it?"

The scribe replied, "'You shall love the Lord your
God with all your heart, with all your soul, with all your
strength, and with all your mind,' and 'your neighbor as
yourself'" (Luke 10:26–27). But after Jesus praised his
response, it became apparent that the scribe really wasn't
looking for answers after all; he was looking for an out:
"But he, wanting to justify himself, said to Jesus, 'And

who is my neighbor?'" (Luke 10:29). He wanted to narrow the scope of his responsibilities so that he could feel better about himself.

His response reminds me of the account I read concerning W. C. Fields, the famous actor and radio personality of an earlier generation. Fields led a rather intemperate life by his own admission. One day not long before he died, a friend found him sitting with a Bible open on his lap, slowly turning its pages. Taken aback by the actor's uncharacteristic interest in the Scriptures, the friend asked, "What are you doing?"

The reply was pure Fields: "Looking for loopholes."

The Lord Jesus left no loopholes in His identification of who constitutes a neighbor. In what has come to be called the parable of the Good Samaritan, religious people (a priest and a Levite) pass by the victim of a mugging and ignore his desperate need. By contrast, a lowly Samaritan comes to the victim's aid (Luke 10:30–37).

Samaritans were despised by the Jews—especially by religious ones, such as the scribe with whom Jesus was conversing. Samaritans were the products of intermarriage of Gentile men to Jewish woman left behind after Assyria's successful invasion in the eight century B.C. of Israel, including its capital, Samaria. The children that came from these unions constituted what the scribe would have called a mongrel race. In Jesus' story, however, it is the Samaritan who allows himself to be inconvenienced and who takes responsibility for the welfare of a man who might have hated him under other circumstances.

Jesus asked the scribe, "So which of these three do you think was neighbor to him who fell among the thieves?" (Luke 10:36).

The scribe could not bring himself to use the word "Samaritan" in his answer, saying instead, "He who showed mercy on him" (Luke 10:37). Jesus then append-ed the command that gives the story its clever and pene-trating surprise ending: "Go and do likewise."

The scribe wanted to know how to determine who belonged in the "neighbor" category. Jesus explained that the critical issue is not trying to *find* one's neighbor but rather *being* a neighbor to those in need. Who is the proper focus of the Golden Rule? Everyone. Nobody is excluded by virtue of not being a neighbor.

TOO BUSY TO LOVE?

Being a neighbor, however, often falls by the wayside in the pace of modern life. A Pennsylvania consulting firm recently released one of those studies estimating the amount of time the average American will spend doing various things over the course of a lifetime. The results are not encouraging. Consider:

- Time spent opening junk mail: eight months
- Time spent sitting at stoplights: six months
- Time spent searching for misplaced objects: one year
- Time spent trying to return phone calls: two years
- Time spent doing housework: four years
- Time spent standing in line: five years

I was disappointed that they didn't tell me how much time I would spend trying to end phone conversa-tions with telemarketers.

Perhaps it is understandable, given the time modern man must allot to secondary matters, that we are tempted to regard other people's needs as additional burdens piled on an already stretched schedule. Understandable . . . but not justifiable.

An ethics professor at an East Coast seminary once asked for volunteers for an extra assignment. When fifteen students raised their hands, the teacher then divided the students into three groups of five each. Each person was given an envelope with individual instructions. The students in the first group were told to proceed immediately across campus to a particular lecture hall; they had fifteen minutes to arrive. Failure to do so would affect their grades. This was called the "High Hurry" group.

A minute or two later he handed out envelopes to five others. Their instructions again were to go to the same location; they, however, were given forty-five minutes to make the trip. After they left, he issued the instructions to the third group, the "Low Hurry" group. They were given three hours to arrive at the destination.

Without telling the students, the teacher had arranged for three people from a local university drama department to encounter them along the way, pretending to be in distress. One actor covered his head with his hands and moaned loudly, as if in great pain. Another appeared on the steps of a campus building, lying face down as if unconscious. Then, on the steps of their destination building, a third drama student was acting out an epileptic seizure.

No one stopped to render aid in the High Hurry group; in the second, two of the five did. In the Low Hurry Group, all five stopped to help. The professor concluded that we have a tendency to allow our schedules to shape our ethics.[1]

We are part of an era in which people seem too pre-occupied to be neighbors. Our own schedules take priority. Yet in refusing to allow ourselves to be inconvenienced, we miss some of life's greatest blessings.

The Lord Jesus, in contrast to so many of us, was never too busy to make time for people in distress. It wasn't that He had nothing pressing on His schedule (as I have heard people suggest). His daily agenda included healing broken bodies and hearts, preaching the gospel to the poor, and proclaiming liberty to the captives (Luke 4:18). While He fulfilled these prophetic assignments, He also worked under severe time constraints. The Lord Jesus had three years to train leaders for a movement that would eventually encompass the globe, yet in the midst of these pursuits He was never too busy for people.

A FACE IN THE CROWD

Once, while on His way to heal a little girl who was lying at death's door, Jesus was touched by a woman with a chronic bleeding problem: "Suddenly, a woman who had a flow of blood for twelve years came from behind and touched the hem of His garment; for she said to herself, 'If only I may touch His garment, I shall be made well.' But Jesus turned around, and when He saw her He said, 'Be of good cheer, daughter; your faith has made you well.' And the woman was made well from that hour" (Matthew 9:20–22).

This encounter, perhaps better than any other in the Gospels, shows how the Lord Jesus looked at people. He had an eye for their needs and an openness to doing something about them. The ill woman forms a prototype of needy people in our world—those who are in search of a neighbor to love them for Christ's sake.

For one thing, the woman is nameless in the account. Her name does not appear in any of the three gospels that feature the story (Matthew 9:20–22; Mark 5:25–34; Luke 8:43–48), either before or after the healing. She was just a face in the crowd to those who were there. Still worse, I imagine she was regarded as an unconscionable interruption by the little girl's father, who considered himself on a life-and-death mission. From his point of view, nothing could have justified stopping Jesus on the way to heal a dying girl, especially to address a long-standing problem. It was as if an ambulance crew on its way to pick up a heart attack victim stopped alongside the road to give advice to someone with arthritis. The bleeding woman's condition appears to have been important only to one other person in the multitude—the Lord Jesus.

Jesus never treated people as interruptions. He never acted as if what He had to do was so important it had to be done this instant. When you get down to cases, very few matters are that crucial. A proper respect for the centrality of the Golden Rule will keep people from just being faces in the crowd around us.

This nameless, hurting woman (remember, for twelve years she had been bleeding, growing weaker and weaker) must have felt hopeless. According to the gospel writers, she had tried everything to improve her condition. She had once possessed a number of assets but had since spent everything she had on medical help (Mark 5:26).

In any case, true medical assistance for the woman's affliction was hard to find in that setting. For example, one rabbinic prescription for a woman with a persistent hemorrhage advised: "Set her in a place where two paths cross, and let her hold a cup of wine in her hand; and let somebody come behind and frighten her, and say, 'Arise from your hemorrhage.'" Not too helpful. Another remedy consisted of drinking a goblet of wine containing a powder compounded from rubber, alum, and garden crocuses. Still another prescription called for carrying the ash of an ostrich's egg in a certain kind of cloth.[2]

To make matters still worse, the woman was an outcast. Not only was her case hopeless, she couldn't even talk about it. It was one of those concerns you didn't mention in polite society. According to Leviticus 15:25, such women could not even take part in public worship, since they were ceremonially unclean. In fact, contact with this woman could have the effect of rendering others unclean, and they could well resent it. That is why her touching of the garment of Jesus was such a courageous maneuver, and why she was so timid in acknowledging her action. She knew Jesus might have been justified in being angry with her.

She was a nameless, hurting, hopeless outcast—and at times, most people feel just like her. If three decades of pastoral work have taught me anything, it is that everybody has a story to tell. They think their story wouldn't be regarded by outsiders as particularly important, so they don't tell it often. But to the one with the story, it is where they live. All of us, at one time or another, feel dreadfully alone. The curse of that is obvious, but the blessing of it is that we recognize and appreciate someone who behaves as a neighbor to us. People who obey the Golden Rule truly stand out— especially if we haven't been much of a neighbor to them.

CHOOSING TO LOVE

The Lord Jesus went out of His way, in fact, to call on us to love people who have already decided not to reciprocate: "But I say to you, love your enemies, bless those who curse you, do good to those who hate you, and pray for those who spitefully use you and persecute you" (Matthew 5:44).

God's Golden Rule—even extending love to enemies—necessarily puts love into the volitional (touching the will) rather than the emotional camp. You probably won't have warm feelings for people who curse you, yet you can choose to extend love to them.

The Lord gives three specific illustrations of how you can choose to express love toward enemies. Love for them ought to affect our speech, our behavior, and our prayer lives: "Bless . . . do good . . . pray" (Matthew 5:44).

. . . BY BLESSING ENEMIES

First, we are to *bless* our enemies. Blessing our enemies means speaking well of them, not just avoiding hostile words about them. We cannot decide how we will feel toward people who detest us, but we can decide what we will say to them (and about them). Robert E. Lee once showed that he knew the difference between feeling warmly toward someone and doing what is good toward him. Confederate President Jefferson Davis asked Lee what he thought of a certain officer in the army, as Davis was looking for a trustworthy man to fill an important place. Lee gave the officer an excellent recommendation and Davis immediately promoted the officer to the empty post. One of Lee's friends, overhearing the conversation, asked the general if he knew that the officer in question had said some very bitter things against Lee. "I know," Lee replied, "but I was not asked for the officer's opinion of me, but for my opinion of him."[3]

... BY DOING GOOD TO ENEMIES

We cannot manufacture warm feelings for people who disregard us, but we can decide to return kindness to them instead of harm. By doing so, we not only obey the Golden Rule, we also avoid the pitfall of having our inner lives diminished, for retaliation makes us smaller people inside.

Booker T. Washington was born in a slave cabin in Virginia a few years before the Civil War. Through incredible diligence and devotion, he became a noted educator and the founder of Tuskegee Institute. Along the way he suffered a great deal of abuse. Late in life he found an excellent opportunity to get even with a man who once had been extremely cruel to him. One of his friends urged that he take advantage of the chance to make this man's life difficult. When Washington refused, his friend wanted to know why he turned down such a choice opportunity for revenge. He said, "I will not let another human being reduce my soul to the level of hatred."[4] Dr. Washington had it right. Loving others as ourselves enlarges our souls; hatred diminishes them.

... BY PRAYING FOR ENEMIES

Praying for our enemies can often do more than simply improve their condition. It can change our attitudes toward them. We begin to care and think about their needs. Sometimes, it does even more than change attitudes. The 1989 annual report of the Southern Baptist Foreign Mission Board included the story of one church's response to tragedy. In the Democratic Republic of the Congo (called Zaire at the time), a group of fanatical Muslims put a series of Christian churches to the torch one Saturday night. The next morning, one of the arsonists passed by the ruins of one of the burned churches and noted that Christians were gathering for worship amid the ashes.

Intrigued, the young man paused to listen to their prayers. Taking Matthew 5:44 seriously, these believers did not pray for revenge, but that God would forgive those who had burned their building. The Holy Spirit used this expression of obedience to the Golden Rule to bring the observer to Christ. Now he gives his testimony in churches throughout the area—including some of those he helped burn.[5] Kindness is a language that the deaf can hear and the blind can read—and even enemies can appreciate.

LOVING NEIGHBORS NEAR AND FAR

My Neighbor in Somalia

The term *neighbor* simply means "the other guy." In the framework of first century Jewish culture, Jesus' insistence that we should love our neighbors as ourselves didn't eliminate anyone. He obviously did not intend that we should love the people on our block but be indifferent to people at a distance.

Through prayer and involvement in world missions, we can convey God's love to our neighbors all over the globe. He died for the dirt farmer in Somalia and the cab driver in Bombay just as much as He did for the affluent North American. Fulfilling the Golden Rule to distant neighbors means assuming a degree of personal responsibility in loving the world for Christ's sake. That means placing yourself in one or more of several categories with respect to extending God's love globally.

THOSE WHO GO

One category is "those who go." Going personally is much more feasible than most people realize. Yes, I know all the standard reasons that people don't go: I have a family to raise, I'm too old, I need special training, and so on. Every day, however, people just like you and me find that these reasons can be overcome.

For one thing, you don't have to make a career of mission work. You can contribute your labors during vacations. Many churches send work teams to mission fields, giving people an opportunity to share Christ's love without committing themselves to years of training and fund-raising.

If your short-term experiences raise a desire to serve for a longer period, you can consider taking an early retirement to get involved in missions work, either on a short- or long-term basis. Some perceptive observers have noted that most people don't die of old age, they die of retirement. I read somewhere that half of the men retiring in the state of New York die within two years. With lots of time and little to do, retirees can find themselves idle, without a sense of purpose. Indeed, a conventional, passive retirement can be a disaster rather than a blessing.

If you're a long way from retirement, consider using

the time between now and then to get some training. Even if you can't attend a Bible college or seminary, you can pursue some basic credentials through distance learning, correspondence courses, and the Internet.

Retirement ought to be a time in which we are able to do what we want to do instead of simply what we must do. For Christians, it makes sense to plan for a time that is filled with contributions to the extension of the love of Christ, whether through the local church or some other ministry. The work has eternal consequences and eternal rewards for those who participate in it.

It is true, however, that not everyone can go. You may choose to be a part of the next category.

THOSE WHO HELP THOSE WHO GO

Loving people at a distance works best when we support those who go with prayer and practical help. Such help can take many forms: "care packages" sent abroad, phone calls, and encouraging notes, for instance. And we can develop cross-cultural friendships here at home. Such friendships help us understand the ministry of missionaries, may yield natural opportunities to express one's faith, and even help missionaries in their work.

A Chicago businessman once called his wife to get approval for him to bring home a visiting foreign guest for dinner. With three children in school and one preschooler, she had plenty of reasons to beg off entertaining strangers, but this Christian woman knew the potential of showing love to people for Christ's sake. The meal turned out to be a lovely time. The foreigner, an important Spanish official, never forgot the hospitality and kindness of that Christian home.

Years later, some friends of this hospitable family found themselves in Spain as missionaries. At one point, their work was hindered by government red tape. When the Spanish official received word that the missionaries were friends of the Chicago couple who had extended kindness to him, he used his influence to remove the hindrances. An evangelical church exists today in that province of Spain, due in part to love extended through a simple evening meal.[6] You never know what you can do if you use your home to make friends for Jesus Christ and to create a global vision in your family. Just about every Christian can love a distant neighbor this way.

THOSE WHO PRAY FOR THOSE WHO GO

Every Christian can love people at a distance through prayer. Every Christian can and should pray. F. B. Meyer once insisted that, "The Christian people of our charge should come to understand that they are not a company of invalids, to be wheeled about, or fed by hand, cosseted, nursed, and comforted, the minister being the Head Physician and Nurse; but a garrison in an enemy's country, every soldier of which should have some post or duty, at which he should be prepared to make any sacrifice rather than quitting."[7] A post every Christian ought to occupy is that of prayer warrior.

The work of missions is not supposed to overwhelm us; it is supposed to turn our hopes to the one person who is big enough to get the job done. The harvest is His harvest, not ours; but He has told us to pray that recruits might be found to extend God's love to the ends of the earth. Jesus said, "Pray the Lord of the harvest to send out laborers into His harvest" (Matthew 9:38).

In the previous chapter, I mentioned the missionary William Carey, a man whose accomplishments are legendary. This self-taught cobbler-turned-linguist labored in India for forty-two years without a furlough and set an amazing example of single-minded devotion to ministry. When Carey landed in Serampore, only a few hundred missionaries were working in the world. Within twenty years of his arrival in India, however, mission activity exploded.

Books have been written about Carey. Libraries, seminaries, and foundations have been named for him, and rightly so. Little notice, however, has been taken of his sister. The omission is probably understandable. She was an invalid, almost totally paralyzed for fifty-two years. But she occupied her post of duty in her brother's ministry, though at a distance. She prayed for his mission tasks.

He wrote to her detailing his struggles in writing grammar books, primers, and dictionaries, and in producing Bibles. He described the challenges of founding newspapers and schools, of training teachers, beginning churches, and educating church leaders. And as William Carey worked, his bedridden sister in London lifted those details to the Lord in prayer.[8] From heaven's point of view, she no doubt shares in the credit, and there is plenty of credit to be shared.

THOSE WHO SEND THOSE WHO GO

Similarly, everyone can help send those who are trying to go themselves. Cards and letters of encouragement, gifts for the kids at Christmas, or a phone call from time to time all remind missionaries that others are in the fight with them.

Financial support is important, too. You may attend a church that uses a portion of your regular weekly giving to support missionaries. I hope you do. However, most missionaries also have a base of individual and family support that enables them to stay on the field. After you supply your local church, you will probably find that you have some money left that can be used to support an individual missionary or two. A few dollars a month in the right hands can create tremendous physical and spiritual blessings for people; and if the Western world doesn't shoulder a sizable share of the load, who will?

We sometimes forget the many needs of the world's inhabitants; and as Americans, we forget our bounty. If we liken the world to a community of a hundred people, about eighty of them would be illiterate. One would have a college education. About fifty would be suffering the effects of a poor diet, and almost eighty would live in what by Western standards would be considered unfit housing. In this representative village, six would be Americans who would have nearly half of the entire income of the community.

Biblically speaking, such high privilege creates high responsibility. "For everyone to whom much is given, from him much will be required," Jesus declared, "and to whom much has been committed, of him they will ask the more" (Luke 12:48). If you can go, go. If you can't go, make friends with, pray for, and financially support those who do. Prove yourself to be a neighbor to distant people for whom Christ died.

NOTES

1. James S. Hewett, ed., "The Good Samaritan and Fast Lane Religious Leaders," *Parables, Etc.,* May 1986, 1.

2. William Barclay, *The Gospel of Matthew* (Philadelphia: Westminster, 1975), 1:346.

3. Charles B. Flood, *Lee: The Last Years,* quoted in James S. Hewett, ed., *Illustrations Unlimited* (Wheaton, Ill.: Tyndale, 1988), 222.

4. S. I. McMillen, *None of These Diseases* (Old Tappan, N.J.: Revell, 1963), 69.

5. As told in James S. Hewett, "Compassionate Prayers," *Pastor's Story File,* August 1991, 3.

6. As told in Michael P. Green, *Illustrations for Biblical Preaching* (Grand Rapids: Baker, 1989), 196–97.

7. Ibid., 64.

8. Warren Myers with Ruth Myers, *Pray: How to be Effective in Prayer* (Colorado Springs: NavPress, 1983), xv–xvii.

Chapter Four

SHOULD I WORK
AT LOVING MYSELF?

*D*on Shula, former coach of the Miami Dolphins pro football team, used to tell the story on himself about how he and his wife once vacationed in a seaside town in Maine. They had gone to the small community mostly because they felt it was a place where the well-known coach might be able to enjoy a measure of anonymity.

One rainy night while they were in town, the Shulas decided to take in a movie. When Don and his wife walked into the small theater, however, the moviegoers already present stood and began to applaud enthusiastically. The famous coach whispered to his wife, "I guess there's no place we can go where people won't recognize me."

When they sat down, Shula shook hands with a man on their row and said, "I'm surprised that you knew who I am."

The man looked at him and replied, "I'm sorry—am

I supposed to know who you are? We're just glad you came in because the manager said he wasn't going to start the movie unless there were at least ten people here."[1]

To paraphrase Job, mankind comes forth from the womb speaking ego. We have an alarming capacity to see the world only from our own perspective. The Lord Jesus wisely took advantage of our egocentricity when He commanded, "Love your neighbor as yourself." The final two words are intended to provide a simple analogy, unmistakable and inescapable, so that we might know the degree of commitment to others He expects from us.

Instead, the phrase has produced an entire body of literature which uses philology (the study of words), theology, psychology, and other-ologies to explain how the first step in loving others is to come to an appreciation of oneself. It is unreasonable and unrealistic, we are told, to expect people who have low self-esteem to love others. First, they must rehabilitate themselves (or be rehabilitated by specialists) so that they can love themselves. Then and only then will they be free to love other people.

Only the rampant narcissism of our day could have produced such a strange and esoteric twist to the simple command to "love your neighbor." That is not to say that people who have been abused and mistreated find it a simple thing to obey the Golden Rule. For that matter, who does? All people suffer in varying degrees from mistreatment by others. The way out of that pit, however, is not to turn inward and postpone one's obedience until the day all emotional pains are gone. The solution is to get our eyes off ourselves and practice *agape* love toward others as a response to divine command. We are to love others even if we have not and may not receive love from them. When we love this way, we find our own problems placed in proper perspective.

DO WE FIRST NEED EMOTIONAL HEALING?

Part of the confusion about self-love comes from the faulty definition of love we looked at in chapter 2. If loving your neighbor is fundamentally emotional, as the world so consistently tells us, then some sort of attempt at emotional healing might be in order.

If loving someone is seeking his welfare, however, then virtually all people already love themselves in the sense the Lord Jesus assumed in giving the Golden Rule. We all work regularly to provide for our physical and emotional health and comfort. In fact, most people focus too narrowly on loving themselves; that is why the Golden Rule is necessary in the first place.

We should not interpret Jesus' words as meaning, "Love your neighbor as you would love yourself if you were emotionally healthy." Rather, we should understand it as, "Love your neighbor with the same consistency and intensity that you use in looking out for your own basic needs every day."

When I get up in the morning, I begin immediately to engage in those activities that promote my welfare. I brush my teeth in order to avoid pain, offensive breath, and tooth decay. I wash my body and comb my hair so that people do not look (or sniff) at me strangely as I go about my business. I eat food virtually every day. I clothe myself, taking due regard not only for appearance but also for comfort. I try to allow myself adequate rest. I seek out medical help when it is needed. These are all activities I consider fundamental to my well-being. I do them whether I feel energetic or lethargic. Such activities form irrefutable evidences of self-love, and they appear in virtually every human life.

The God of heaven sees what we do every day to take care of ourselves. The same loving treatment we consistently exhibit toward ourselves we must learn to exercise toward others. Happily for us, He not only commands that we love others, He also gives us the model for doing so in His own actions.

GOD'S MODEL FOR LOVING OTHERS

When God brought Israel out of Egypt, He was redeeming a nation of slaves. They had suffered abuse of the worst sort for four centuries. When the nation found itself on the east side of the Jordan River, Moses gave his farewell address—what we call the book of Deuteronomy—to the people so that they might see how God's love works.

Moses told Israel to avoid legal entanglements with the pagan nations they were displacing. His rationale? Israel, by making treaties with the peoples around it, would lose its distinctiveness as a people—a distinctiveness brought about by the love of God. God's love toward Israel, described in Deuteronomy 7:6–9, embodies four qualities that model His own love and define how His people are to love others.

GOD'S LOVE EXALTS

God's love is exalting. That is, God continually looks for ways to build up and make the one He loves a better person. Moses told Israel, "The Lord your God has chosen you to be a people for Himself, a special treasure above all the peoples on the face of the earth" (Deuteronomy 7:6). I have been asked quite often through the years, "Why did God choose Israel?" The answer people are looking for is almost always the wrong one. By the question, they mean "What was it about the children of Israel that attracted God to them?"

That's the wrong question. God didn't choose them because of what they were; He chose them because of what He wanted them to be. God chose them in order to exalt them. His love invariably lifts people. Because He loves me, I am a better person. Yes, I am justified through Christ and given eternal life, but His love means even more than that. His love lifts and improves me in practical ways right now.

Are the people you love becoming better people because you love them? Have you contributed to their exaltation by doing those things that will move them in the right direction? Have you taken a personal interest in people to the point that they know that you want nothing for them except what will make them better? If those things are true, then you are reflecting the exalting nature of God's love in obeying the Golden Rule.

GOD'S LOVE IS PERSISTENT

God's love is not easily overcome by resistance. Moses told God's people, "The Lord did not set His love on you nor choose you because you were more in number than any other people, for you were the least of all peoples" (Deuteronomy 7:7). God didn't choose to set His love on Israel because they were impressive.

So why did He? The text continues, "But because the Lord loves you, and because He would keep the oath which He swore to your fathers" (Deuteronomy 7:8).

Do you see what Moses is telling us in that brief but profound phrase? God didn't choose the people of Israel so much as He chose to love their leaders, the patriarchs—Abraham, Isaac, and Jacob. He loved three men, and because He loved three men, He chose to persist in that love by expressing it toward numberless generations of their offspring. His love is a hard thing to shake. Ours should be too.

Do the people in your life benefit from the consistency of the way you love them? If they do, you have put them in touch with one important characteristic of God's love. Persistent love generally has to be supernatural in origin. Anybody can love people who are nice. God loves us even when we aren't, and He keeps loving us long enough to make us nice.

GOD'S LOVE IS SELF-INITIATING

God's love flows from His character. That is, His love doesn't depend on getting the proper response from the one He loves. He hasn't always received much of a response from Israel, but He has never stopped loving them. God waited a long time to get anything like a response from me, but He never stopped loving me, not for one second. Why is that? Moses explains in Deuteronomy: "The Lord did not set His love on you nor choose you because you were more in number than any other people, for you were the least of all peoples; but because the Lord loves you" (Deuteronomy 7:7–8).

Notice the logic: The Lord set His love on you because the Lord loves you. He loves you because He wants to. There is nothing outside of God that makes Him love anyone. His love comes from inside. It is a love of inwardly born determination. God loves people because He is the kind of person who would be contradicting Himself if He didn't.

Most importantly for us, His love is designed to be imitated. You can tell when you are becoming a better person because your circle of love and concern expands. People enter the world in a state of total self-absorption. When Jesus Christ moves into your life, He begins to develop the love in you that He Himself exhibits. That means that you choose to love people rather than simply respond to their kindness toward you. When Jesus Christ was hanging on a cross, He was not there because the authorities put Him there. Love put Him there—the love that is intrinsic to His nature. He could have resisted the Cross and abandoned His mission of love, but He chose to go (Matthew 26:53–54; John 10:17–18).

GOD'S LOVE IS LIBERATING

God's love always seeks to make its object independent in the right sense. Moses quotes God's words: "[I] brought you out with a mighty hand, and redeemed you from the house of bondage" (Deuteronomy 7:8). What a world of truth is taught in these brief expressions! To redeem is to liberate—to pay a price to buy a slave's freedom. *Redeem* is a word that often appears in connection with Israel's exodus from Egypt. God freed the Jewish slaves from Egyptian bondage and gave them the Passover celebration to remember it by. The Lord's Table, one of the central ordinances of the Christian church, originated as a Passover meal. It is the time when we pause to contemplate the price paid for our redemption, a price of blood and suffering.

But when God loves people, He doesn't smother them. He lets them go. While He wants us to love Him in return, He does not compel our love. He knows that love that is not freely extended isn't worth much.

But God is not merely a passive liberator, either. He doesn't wash His hands of us. His release is designed to change us, to make us more like Christ His Son. As a result, while God doesn't compel, He does arrange things in our experience so that we will begin to look outward—that is, to see the Golden Rule as our lifestyle and devotion to its Author as our passion.

Those arrangements don't feel comfortable at first. A. B. Simpson, the father of the Christian and Missionary Alliance, wrote about this:

> If we would be enlarged, we must accept all that God sends us to develop and expand our spiritual life. We are so content to abide at the old level that God often has to compel us to rise higher by bringing us face to face with situations that we cannot meet without much greater measures of His grace. It is as though He had to send a tidal wave to flood the lowlands where we dwell to compel us to move into the hills beyond. God, like the mother bird, sometimes has to break up the comfortable, downy nest, letting us drop into empty space. There we must either learn to use an entirely new and higher method of support or sink into failure and loss.[2]

Obedience to the Golden Rule takes some getting used to. It will stretch us spiritually so that we learn a holy dependence upon God to help us love people. God's love is not painless; but it is liberating, even in the most confining environment.

Until the end of the communist-led Soviet Union in 1989, the underground church there suffered terribly. The Cold War included sending Christians to labor camps to serve long prison terms. Often they were accused of being insane because of their belief in a deity. In the camps they experienced awful conditions: little sanitation, inadequate food and shelter, and almost no medical care. Still worse, camp inmates, often rough and disagreeable people, displayed open hostility toward the Christians' faith.

Many of the believers held in the gulag, however, refused to be crushed under their burdens. Realizing that the hatred they suffered was largely due to the internal misery of those who detested them, they put the Golden Rule into action in their terrible environment. An inmate and persecutor named Kozlov observed the behavior of these Christians. The general prison population cursed their environment and each other, but "the Christians (often with sentences of twenty to twenty-five years) did not despair. One could see Christ reflected in their faces. Their pure, upright life, deep faith and devotion to God, their gentleness and their wonderful manliness, became a shining example of real life for thousands."[3]

Kozlov did more than write about those Christian prisoners. He became a believer in their Lord and a leader in His church. Their behavioral modeling of kindness and compassion overcame his own initial skepticism. The darker the surroundings, the more visible and compelling Christ's love becomes, and the more Christ-like those who exhibit it.

HOW GOD'S LOVE FREES US

GOD'S CHISEL AT WORK

In the 1960s, I was part of a missionary basketball team that toured the South Pacific and Far East. Part of our tour took us to Thailand, where in between games we toured some of the wonders of that country. On one side trip, our hosts took us to see the temple of the Golden Buddha. The temple itself is small, but what is inside is striking—a ten-foot-tall statue of Buddha made out of solid gold, weighing two and a half tons.

What is even more amazing is how this icon came to see the light of day. Back in 1957, the statue was covered with clay. Under eight inches of clay lay a statue of solid gold. One day somebody decided to move the statue from one building to another. When the crane operator began to lift the object, its cables seemed to strain at this supposedly clay statue. As the procedure continued, the clay began to crack. To further complicate matters, rain began falling. The moving process was stopped, and the statue was covered with a tarpaulin overnight.

When the movers returned in the evening to check on the statue's condition, they lifted the tarp and peered inside with a flashlight. The observers noticed a reflection; was there some shiny metal underneath? They summoned an artisan with a chisel. Eventually he uncovered one of the largest gold objects in the world, conservatively estimated to be worth 200 million dollars.

So how did a golden statue come to be covered with hard clay? No one knows for sure, but one reasonable hypothesis connects it with an invasion of Thailand by the Burmese many centuries ago. A group of Thais, concerned that their golden statue would be cut up and carted away by the invaders, covered it in clay so that its great value would not be recognized. Unfortunately, all of them (according to the theory) were slaughtered by the Burmese, so there was no one left to reveal its value.

Christians are a lot like that statue. At the moment of your conversion and mine, God puts something immensely valuable inside us; namely, the life of Christ. But the sins and faults we bring into our Christian experience keep that life from being clearly seen at first. Christian growth is the Holy Spirit's process of chiseling away what is wrong so that the beauty of the life of Christ can be seen by others. That's what He wants to do with you and me, and Christ's life is never more evident than when we demonstrate and express His love toward people.

SEEING "THE LIGHT AND LOVE OF CHRIST"

Pete Maravich, one of the greatest basketball players of all time, became a Christian believer late in his brief life. (He died of a heart attack at age forty.) In his autobiography, he told how he had become totally wrapped up in himself and what a difference it made when he came to know the Lord Jesus:

> One of the first things I realized after I had settled things with God was the difference it made to be dedicated to something other than myself. Everything I had done since childhood was for selfish reasons, such as bringing adoration to myself, finding acceptance among my peers, and gratifying my ego. This selfishness had led to emptiness and no conventional way out of my self-centered way of life. Trying to please others had brought

me frustration, a drinking habit, and a love of material possessions. I had gone to the brink of self-destruction. After my conversion that special night in Metairie, Louisiana, I turned full circle. All the fame and fortune I had accumulated looked extremely pale when compared to the abundance of Christ in me. I was driven by a desire to please God because of the newness of life I had received from him. The fears I had once possessed were wiped away; I became much more open to people. The solemn moods that had plagued me began to disappear. Instead my life was now filled with the light and love of Christ.[4]

Many less famous people can tell of similar experiences. Practicing the Golden Rule helps to make us and the people we love truly free, assuming that we practice it with the proper intensity and direction.

A LOVE THAT UNDERSTANDS

Knowing how to love yourself isn't the problem most people have in obeying the Golden Rule. The real challenge is understanding how to help your neighbor. Loving people as yourself requires a special kind of knowledge—not the academic kind, but the empathetic kind. We have to try to understand how the other person thinks so that our actions encourage and edify rather than crush and ignore. The God of heaven set the example here by becoming a Man so that He could be a merciful and faithful High Priest (Hebrews 4:15).

Not thinking about how things look from the perspective of others can create terrible hurts, even when good intentions are present. When I was in college, I was involved in what observers might have termed a small awakening on campus. A lot of my friends were turning to Christ. I came home one evening from a study hall to discover that there were thirteen new Christians in my fraternity house, a place which could not have been regarded (up to that point, at least) as a beacon of spiritual truth.

In their zeal to share their faith, some of the young Christians on campus went home as soon as possible to explain to their parents what had happened to them. With very few exceptions, their announcements were not received as they had hoped. Instead of being encouraged, the students returned to campus deflated, telling how their parents seemed to resent their newfound faith.

In some cases, at least, the problem might have been avoided if the students had been looking at their own experience through their parents' eyes. From the students' point of view, they were telling about their conversion—a new and exciting turning point in their lives. From the parents' point of view, they were hearing an indictment of the spiritual training they had provided during their children's formative years (or even a condemnation of themselves).

In some cases, it wouldn't have mattered. No matter how tactful we are, spiritual truth does divide (Matthew 10:34–36). God does not require that we agree with others, however, only that we care enough to try and understand them. We often have to endure some pain ourselves to do that effectively.

Pastor and author Don Baker recalled once helping a couple in pain; they had just lost their firstborn in childbirth.

Don had been asked to call on them by one of his

church members. Before he arrived, the couple was alone in the hospital room when their own pastor came in. He took a seat and asked, "What sin is God punishing you for?" They could not reply because of shock at his insensitivity.

Shortly afterward, Don arrived and introduced himself. He said to them, "I'm sorry you've lost your baby, but I do know how you feel." For a moment they became angry—until he added, "We lost our little baby too."

Don accompanied the grieving parents to the cemetery, where he conducted a brief graveside ceremony. While there, he showed them his own child's grave and began the long process of helping them see beyond their hurts. Eventually they were able to face all the potentialities of having another baby, which they did. The couple expressed their gratitude by saying, "Thank you for entering into our sorrow with us."[5]

That is what obedience to the Golden Rule sometimes requires. When we enter other people's pain, we tread a well-worn and holy path. Jesus Christ has already been there, and walking in His steps not only helps us minister to others, but also begins to free us from our own obsession with self.

NOTES

1. John Ortberg, "Attitudes," Willowcreek Community Church (Barrington, Ill.). Seeds Tape Ministry #M9733, as quoted in Raymond McHenry, ed., *In Other Words,* 8, no. 2 (Spring 1998): 2.

2. A. B. Simpson, *A Larger Christian Life,* as quoted in *Leadership* [computer disk]. Available from the Autoillustrator, P.O. Box 50556, Greeley, CO., 80631.

3. Janice A. Broun, "Evangelism in the U.S.S.R.," *Christianity Today,* 21 June 1974, 14.

4. Pete Maravich, *Heir to a Dream* (Nashville: Nelson, 1987), 200.
5. Don Baker, *Restoring Broken Relationships* (Eugene, Ore.: Harvest House, 1989), 119.

Chapter Five

THE GOLDEN

PARADOX

*B*laise Pascal, a seventeenth-century Frenchman and one of history's most brilliant minds, was a philosopher, mathematician, and devout Christian believer. He once explained the overarching motive of human behavior:

> All men seek happiness. This is without exception. Whatever different means they employ, they all tend to this end. The cause of some going to war, and of others avoiding it, is the same desire in both, attended with different views. The will never takes the least step but to this object. This is the motive of every action of every man, even of those who hang themselves.[1]

Apparently God built a longing for joy into the human condition. Try as we might to do otherwise, we virtually always behave in a manner that we think (whether we are right or wrong) will produce short- or long-term happiness for us. The pains that are part of human experience do not come because we desire happiness, but because we so often choose faulty ways of obtaining it.

LOOKING FOR HAPPINESS

God's intention has always been that we find our happiness in Him: in the goodness of His person, in the glories of His attributes, and in carrying out His purposes in the world. The latter, of course, includes obedience to the Golden Rule. When people spurn or ignore His ways, however, they seek fulfillment in places that inevitably disappoint. As a result, a large portion of the human race flounders about in confusion and boredom. We are like the central character in the story told by presidential candidate Thomas E. Dewey. After he was defeated in the 1948 presidential race, Dewey described himself as sympathetic to the man who had passed out from excessive drinking at a wake. He was laid in a spare coffin so he could sleep off the effects of his inebriation. When he woke up and realized where he was, he was confronted by contradictory impulses. He asked himself, "If I am alive, why am I in this coffin? And if I'm dead, why do I have to go to the bathroom?"[2] Man knows he isn't dead, but he isn't quite sure why he is alive.

Even people whom the world regards as outstanding feel the emptiness of life without God—whether or not they would even acknowledge His existence. George Sanders won an Oscar for his portrayal of urbane theater critic Addison DeWitt in the 1950 film *All About Eve.* Unable to find personal fulfillment to match his professional success, Sanders checked into a hotel near Barcelona in 1972 and swallowed five tubes of Nembutal. His suicide note began: "Dear World. I am leaving because I am bored."[3]

Several years ago the internationally known political cartoonist Ralph Barton also committed suicide. Pinned to his pillow was a note: "I have had few difficulties, many friends, great successes; I have gone from wife to wife, and from house to house, visited great countries of the world, but I am fed up with inventing devices to fill up 24 hours of the day."[4]

C. S. Lewis insisted that because man's pursuit of happiness has gone awry he too readily accepts secondary delights, only to discover too late their inadequacies: "We are half-hearted creatures, fooling about with drink and sex and ambition when infinite joy is offered us, like an ignorant child who wants to go on making mud pies in a slum because he cannot imagine what is meant by the offer of a holiday at the sea."[5] Because our substitute pleasures are so pitiful, a pleasure-obsessed experience is the most boring life of all. By contrast, loving God supremely and others as ourselves produces a series of challenges and benefits that keep life rich and interesting.

THE HAPPY PARADOX

Indeed, when it comes to loving people, God has built into life what one might call a golden paradox: when we concentrate on loving, sacrificial acts for others, we find ourselves blessed—and loved—in the process. As Karl Meninger of the Mayo Clinic wrote, "Love cures people—both the ones who give it and the ones who receive it."[6]

The returned blessings usually develop over a period

of time in the form of godly character and pleasure at seeing changes in our lives and the lives of others. Sometimes those blessings are realized quickly and in tangible ways. One day during the Christmas season a woman we'll call Ellen read an unusual letter to the editor in the local newspaper. "Is there any place where we can borrow a little boy three or four years old for the Christmas holidays?" the letter began. "We have a nice home and would take wonderful care of him and bring him back safe and sound. We used to have a little boy, but he couldn't stay, and we miss him so when Christmas comes."

The words brought her up short. Being the widowed mother of a four-year-old boy herself, she was again briefly captured by the memories of her husband, a man who had died while serving in the military. The grief had lasted a long time. Only now could this widow bring herself to enter into the pain of others, such as that of the family who was appealing for the Christmas "loan" of a four-year-old.

Ellen answered the letter and discovered that the writer was a widower who lived with his mother. He had lost his own wife and young son only months before. She decided to fulfill the request. Later, she explained, "That Christmas, my son and I shared a joyous day with the widower and his mother. Together, we found a happiness that we doubted would ever return. But the best part is that this joy was mine to keep throughout the years and for each of the Christmases since. You see, the man who wrote the letter, months later, became my husband."[7]

While not everyone finds such an obvious or grand reward from the golden paradox, most will come to realize that the world's happiest people are those who obey the Golden Rule and invest themselves in others. There is more than one man's opinion to back up that assertion. Bernard Rimland, a psychologist at the Institute for Child Behavior Research in San Diego, developed a way of evaluating the thesis. He asked 216 people to take a simple written test. Each wrote down the names of about ten people they knew well, then rated them in two areas: (1) were they happy or unhappy? and (2) were they selfish or unselfish? Rimland defined selfishness as "a stable tendency to devote one's time and resources to one's own interests and welfare—and an unwillingness to inconvenience oneself for others."

When he added up the cases of the 1,988 people rated by test participants, he found that 827—far and away the largest response—fell into the happy and unselfish category. In fact, nearly all of the people described as happy also were described as unselfish. The psychologist termed this "the altruism paradox": those who invest in others find happiness themselves.

Rimland's concluding advice? Do unto others as you would have them do unto you.[8] Sort of has a familiar ring to it.

You probably don't need a formal psychological study to convince yourself of this. If you think about it, you will remember times in your own life when you have been richly blessed in blessing others. Dee Taylor recalls learning this principle as a teen by watching her mother. The two of them were grocery shopping in a neighborhood store when she noticed a family enter. The three looked to be a mother, daughter, and grand-daughter. They were apparently not well off; their clothing was worn, though clean.

When Dee and her mother arrived at the checkout counter, the clerk was already beginning to ring up this family's groceries. The older woman asked periodically during the process for a subtotal, as she only had so much to spend. Since this took a while, others in line begin to express impatience. To make matters worse, when the clerk did the final total, the woman discovered that she did not have enough money and began to point at different items to be put back. Dee remembers what happened next:

> My mother reached in her purse, pulled out a twenty dollar bill and handed it to the woman. The woman looked very surprised and said, "I can't take that!" My mother looked directly at the woman and quietly replied, "Yes, you most certainly can. Consider it a gift. There's nothing in that cart you don't really need, so please accept it." The woman then reached out and took the money, squeezing my mom's hand for just a moment, and with tears running down her cheeks, said, "Thank you very much. No one's ever done nothin' like this for me before."
>
> I know I left the store with tears in my eyes, and it is something I will cherish forever. You see, my parents raised six children and didn't have a whole lot of money themselves, although I can never remember wanting for anything. I'm very happy to say that I inherited her caring heart. I have given selflessly before, and there is not a better feeling in the whole world![9]

You may have similar fond memories in your own experience; I hope you do. Be assured that such experiences are not random episodes. God wants you and me to discover for ourselves that He cannot be outgiven. The psalmist lauded God by saying of His children, "They are abundantly satisfied with the fullness of Your house, and You give them drink from the river of Your pleasures" (Psalm 36:8). He wants us to rejoice not only in what kindness does for others, but in what it does for us as well.

THE FLIP SIDE

Not too surprisingly, a paradox exists on the other side of things too. While selfish people by definition are devoted to producing their own happiness, they rarely feel happy. Of the nearly two thousand people who were rated in Dr. Rimland's study, participants described only 4 percent of the people they knew (seventy-eight individuals) as happy and selfish. From the perspective of others, at least, selfish people seem to make themselves happy less often than people who work at extending kindness to others.

Self-centeredness commonly leads to more than simple unhappiness, however; it often produces sorrow and tragedy. Indeed, fixation on the self has a way of producing just the opposite of what the selfish person wants.

Several years ago the president of the American Association of Forensic Scientists, Dr. Don Harper Mills, reported during the organization's annual awards ceremony about a Denver medical examiner called in to determine the cause of death of a young man. Many thought Ronald Opus died from a stray shotgun wound to the head. But the examiner uncovered much more than that.

The body had been recovered from a safety net erected to protect window washers working on the eighth floor of the tall building where Opus had lived. It seems that he had leaped from the top of the building in a suicide attempt (a note was left), but received a shotgun blast as he passed an open window on the ninth floor. The probability of someone shooting Opus at that precise instant was slim, of course. Yet it happened.

In the ordinary course of things, a person who attempts suicide is responsible for his own death. But the shotgun blast complicated things—and so did the safety net. Opus was caught by a net that would have (in the ordinary course of events) saved his life. The medical examiner thus concluded that he probably was investigating a homicide, not a suicide.

Investigators soon traced the shotgun blast to a room occupied by an elderly couple who had been in the middle of a marital disagreement when the gun discharged. The husband had pointed the gun at his wife, but was so upset by their discussion that his aim was spoiled. He thus missed his wife when he pulled the trigger, the pellets from the shot leaving the room through the open window.

Legally, Dr. Mills explained, when one intends to kill one person but instead kills another, he is guilty of the murder of the unintended victim. When confronted with the possibility of being charged with murder, however, both the elderly man and his wife insisted that neither knew that the shotgun was loaded. The man explained that it was his long-standing habit to threaten his wife with the unloaded shotgun when they were at odds. He had no intention of harming her or anyone else. This led the medical examiner to consider that the killing of Opus was probably accidental. That is, the gun had been accidentally loaded without the knowledge of the elderly couple.

At this point came another amazing twist. It turned out that neighbors had observed the elderly couple's son loading the shotgun about six weeks prior to the fatal accident. It seems that the son, one Ronald Opus, had been informed by his mother that she was cutting off his financial support. Ronald apparently loaded the gun in the hopes that his father would accidentally shoot his mother in one of their recurring arguments, thus removing his financial problems. As the weeks had passed and nothing had transpired, the son had grown despondent over his father's inactivity. Finally he chose to leap to his death—only to be killed by a shotgun blast on the way down. The medical examiner closed the case as a suicide.[10] The selfish son had been indirectly responsible for his own death.

Although that's an uncommon story, it's quite common to have selfish acts backfire. The outcome rarely is death, but the consequences almost always are bad. Those who seek to advance themselves at the expense of others find misery and discontent along the way. "Whoever digs a pit will fall into it, and he who rolls a stone will have it roll back on him," Solomon wrote (Proverbs 26:27). To put it in terms of another biblical metaphor, we reap what we sow . . . for good or ill.

IS CHRISTIANITY PURE UNSELFISHNESS?

Not everyone is comfortable with findings like those of the Institute for Child Behavior Research in San Diego (Dr. Rimland's study showing unselfish people were happier with their lives than were selfish people). One school of thought says Christians should always behave altruistically—in ways utterly free of self-interest.

If we extend kindness to others, proponents say, with the hope that we will be blessed in the process, what would ordinarily be an ethical action is spoiled due to our ulterior motive: wanting something in return.

In the Scriptures, however, God routinely attaches benefits (either explicitly or by inference) to obedience of His commandments. Note the four examples in the following chart:

BENEFITS TO OBEYING HIS COMMANDMENTS

	Command	Benefit
Exodus 20:12	"Honor your father and your mother	…that your days may be long upon the land."
Ephesians 6:7–8	"With good will [do] service, as to the Lord, and not to men	…knowing that whatever good anyone does, he will receive the same from the Lord."
Hebrews 11:26	"[Moses esteemed] the reproach of Christ greater riches than the treasures in Egypt	…for he looked to the reward."
Philippians 4:6–7	"Be anxious for nothing, but in everything by prayer and supplication, with thanksgiving, let your requests be made known to God	…and the peace of God, which surpasses all understanding, will guard your hearts and minds through Christ Jesus."

Hundreds of such connections exist in God's Word. God is under no obligation to attach motivations like these, of course. He does so because He knows us well, and because He is a gracious God. He understands that half the time we don't fully grasp our own motives, and He wants to give us lots of reasons to do good. He lets us know that He will bless us for doing what we ought to do anyway—just because He commands it. If we find it impossible to love others simply because He says so, we can at least begin by recognizing that if we love them we will find ourselves benefited.

The strange concern about avoiding blessings for ourselves is a comparatively recent phenomenon, according to C. S. Lewis:

> If you asked twenty good men today what they thought the highest of the virtues, nineteen of them would reply, Unselfishness. But if you asked almost any of the great Christians of old he would have replied, Love. You see what has happened? A negative term has been substituted for a positive, and this is of more than philological importance. . . . The New Testament has lots to say about self-denial, but not about self-denial as an end in itself. We are told to deny ourselves and to take up our crosses in order that we may follow Christ; and nearly every description of what we shall ultimately find if we do so contains an appeal to desire.[11]

The bizarre idea that the value of an action is diminished if the one acting is blessed through it does not come from the Bible. No one responds to God's invitation to believe in Christ in the hopes that others will receive eternal life but not himself. Even the most "selfless" act of human history, Christ dying on the cross, happened because the Lord Jesus looked beyond the short-term pain to what it would bring: "Jesus . . . for *the joy that was set before Him* endured the cross, despising the shame, and has sat down at the right hand of the throne of God" (Hebrews 12:2, italics added). Jesus' present glorification came because He knew that in dying for the world He would in time also be exalted by the Father. In God's scheme of things, no one is ever asked to jettison his own long-term well-being for the sake of another's.

In fact, in loving others we find ourselves more blessed than they: "Remember the words of the Lord Jesus, that He said, 'It is more blessed to give than to receive'" (Acts 20:35). That statement isn't a Christmas cliché; it is a working reality, as those who have put it into practice will testify.

Edie, now a grown woman, remembers Easter 1946 as a special time in her life. She was fourteen, living with two sisters and her mother. Her father had died five years before, and though four older children had already become independent, the family struggled to make ends meet.

About a month before Easter, the family's pastor announced in church that a special offering would be taken on Easter Sunday to assist a poor family. He asked everyone to give sacrificially that day so that the less fortunate could be blessed. So, by doing extra work, conserving their electric power, and eating potatoes for a month, this humble family contributed eighty-seven dollars to the offering for the poor family, rejoicing that they were able to do so much.

Later that same day, however, their joy was dimmed when they discovered that they were the family for

whom the offering had been taken. Edie recalls her
response:

> The minister had brought us the money for the poor
> family, so we must be poor. I didn't like being poor. I
> looked at my dress and worn-out shoes and felt so
> ashamed that I didn't want to go back to church. Every-
> one there probably already knew we were poor! ...
>
> We sat in silence for a long time. Then it got dark, and
> we went to bed. All that week, we girls went to school and
> came home, and no one talked much. Finally on Saturday,
> Mom asked us what we wanted to do with the money.
> What did poor people do with money? We didn't know.
> We'd never known we were poor. We didn't want to go to
> church on Sunday, but Mom said we had to. Although it
> was a sunny day, we didn't talk on the way....
>
> At church we had a missionary speaker. He talked
> about how churches in Africa made buildings out of sun-
> dried bricks, but they need money to buy roofs. He said
> $100 would put a roof on a church. The minister said,
> "Can't we all sacrifice to help these poor people?"
>
> We looked at each other and smiled for the first time
> in a week. Mom reached into her purse and pulled out
> the envelope. She passed it to Darlene. Darlene gave it to
> me, and I handed it to Ocy. Ocy put it in the offering.
> When the offering was counted, the minister announced
> that it was a little over $100. The missionary was excited.
> He hadn't expected such a large offering from our small
> church. He said, "You must have some rich people in this
> church." Suddenly it struck us! We had given $87 of that
> "little over $100." We were the rich family in the church!
> Hadn't the missionary said so? From that day on I've nev-
> er been poor again. I've always remembered how rich I
> am because I have Jesus.[12]

LOVE'S TRANSFORMING POWER

The Christian who desires to make the Golden Rule his or her lifestyle will recognize these things, tuck them away as part of an essential commitment to Christ, and turn his attentions to ministry. God does not want us to carry around a scorecard, attempting to assess the quantity of rewards that will be ours because we have loved others. It is enough to know that there will be some and that the righteous Judge Himself will apportion them. And it is enough to know that we are rich, today.

However, while love does not focus on the returns it brings to the lover, obedience to the Golden Rule produces a subtle but relentless effect. It makes us into people who discover that loving others becomes the increasing passion of our own hearts. It is useful to know that we can behave in a loving way without a great emotional attachment to people, but God is not pleased to have us remain clinical lovers. *Love transforms and lifts the lover equally with the beloved.*

Paul's writings everywhere support this observation. The apostle told the Roman Christians, "Brethren, my heart's desire and prayer to God for Israel is that they may be saved" (Romans 10:1). He was passionate about the salvation of his countrymen, though they had returned little of the extraordinary investment he had made in them. Still, when Paul went to a new city, he went to the synagogue first.

Similarly, he told the Thessalonian believers, "You are our glory and joy" (1 Thessalonians 2:20). The apostle could hardly be considered coolly objective about the people into whom he had poured his life. When you invest time and effort in doing good for others, in time you will always feel differently toward them. "Do not waste your time bothering whether you 'love' your neighbor; act as if you did," wrote C. S. Lewis in *Mere Christianity.* He added:

> As soon as we do this, we find one of the great secrets. When you are behaving as if you loved someone, you will presently come to love him. If you injure someone you dislike, you will find yourself disliking him more. If you do him a good turn, you will find yourself disliking him less.[13]

George Crane, a minister and writer, described in one of his newspaper columns how an angry wife came to him for counsel. She had more in mind than merely ending her miserable marriage. She told him, "I do not only want to get rid of him; I want to get even. Before I divorce him, I want to hurt him as much as he has me."

Crane thought for a moment and then suggested an unorthodox and crafty approach: "Go home and act as if you really love your husband. Tell him how much he means to you. Praise him for every decent trait. Go out of your way to be as kind, considerate, and generous as possible. Spare no efforts to please him, to enjoy him. Make him believe you love him. After you've convinced him of your undying love and that you cannot live without him, then drop the bomb. Tell him that you're getting a divorce. That will really hurt him."

The wife thought it was great counsel. "Beautiful, beautiful," she kept saying. "Will he ever be surprised!"

She went home and went at it with enthusiasm. For two months she was the model of kindness. When she didn't return, Crane called. "Are you ready now to go through with the divorce?"

"Divorce?" she exclaimed. "Never! I discovered I really do love him."

Her "discovery" was a predictable one, as her counselor knew. Loving motions will in time create loving emotions.[14]

Loving others is, in the final analysis, why we are here. Paul Brand, who spent much of his life as a medical missionary to India, told in one of his articles about his mother, who served the Lord for years in a remote area of that country known as the "mountains of death." When he finished his medical training and returned to India, she was sixty-seven, a widow, and in poor health. She fell off a horse and broke several ribs one day and was found by someone on the trail, or she would have died of exposure. Dr. Brand went into the mountains to persuade her to come and live with him in the city. "Mother, you're fortunate someone found you the next day," he began the rehearsed speech. "You could have lain there helpless for days. Shouldn't you think about retiring?"

When his mother said nothing, he marshaled still more arguments. "It's not safe for you to live alone up here where there's no medical help within a day's journey. Surely you realize that even the best of people do sometimes retire before they reach eighty. Why don't you come to Vellore and live with us? We have plenty of good work for you to do, and you'll be much closer to medical help. We'll look after you, Mother."

Dr. Brand thought his arguments compelling, but his mother was unmoved. She had a few arguments of her own. "Paul, you know these mountains. If I leave, who will help the village people? Who will treat their wounds and pull their teeth and teach them about Jesus? When someone comes to take my place, then and only then will I retire. In any case, why preserve this old body if it's not going to be used where God needs me?"

As far as "Granny Brand" was concerned, the discussion was over. Dr. Brand went on to tell how this woman in her youth was considered the belle of London. Young men once competed with each other for her hand, and she was so beautiful at the time that artists used to wait in line to paint her portrait. All that had been lost through years in a harsh environment, he says, but there was a beauty in her that was very real to the people where she worked:

> When she approached, the villagers had rushed out to take her crutches and carry her to a place of honor. In my memory, she is sitting on a low stone wall that circles the village, with people pressing in from all sides. Already they have listened to her praise them for protecting their water supplies and for the orchard that is flourishing on the outskirts. They are listening to what she has to say about the love of God for them. Heads are nodding in encouragement, and deep, searching questions come from the crowd. Mother's own rheumy eyes are shining, and standing beside her I can see what she must be seeing with her failing vision: intent faces gaze with trust and affection on one they have grown to love.
>
> No one else on earth, I realized then, commanded such devotion and love from those villagers. They were looking at a bony, wrinkled old face, but somehow her shrunken tissues had become transparent, and she was all lambent spirit. To them, and to me, she was beautiful.

It was a few years later that my mother died, at the age of 95. Following her instructions, villagers buried her in a simple cotton sheet so that her body would return to the soil and nourish new life. Her spirit, too, lives on, in a church, a clinic, several schools, and in the faces of thousands of villagers across five mountain ranges of South India.[15]

So begin where you can. If you have an emotional attachment to people, it will be easier to do what is good for them. If you don't, do what is good for them anyway. God will use your willingness to obey for their good and for yours.

As I was writing this book, I learned that my cousin, Greta Manolis, was in Baylor Hospital in Dallas. She was there by choice, donating a kidney to her husband's diabetic sister. Greta wanted to express the love of Christ to her sister-in-law, and her unusual action was made possible by a set of remarkably compatible tissues. She is well now (though a little lighter) and looks back on the experience with gratitude. I asked what she had learned from the process. She wrote:

> I got far more from this than I sacrificed. I learned that my God will not forsake me. I learned not to be afraid to ask Him specifically for what I feel I need and I learned to be prepared to go for the ride of a lifetime when He gives me what I ask for. Everything I asked has been given—not necessarily the way I would have done it, but the reality has been much more exciting. And sometimes I think the best part, for me, is my scar. I can physically touch it and remember what God has done for me . . . and for all of us.

NOTES

1. Blaise Pascal, *Pascal's Pensees,* trans. by W. F. Trotter (New York: Dutton, 1958), 113.

2. James S. Hewett, ed., *Illustrations Unlimited* (Wheaton, Ill.: Tyndale, 1988), 212.

3. From the Internet magazine *Salon,* at Salonmagazine.com. Salon features: George Sanders, 9 February 1996 [online]. Available on the World Wide Web: http://www.salonmagazine.com/07/features/sanders2.html. (Contact magazine at Salon.com, 706 Mission Street, San Francisco, CA 94103; telephone 415-882-8720.)

4. Quoted in Josh McDowell, *The Resurrection Factor* (Nashville: Nelson, 1993), 1.

5. C. S. Lewis, *The Weight of Glory and Other Addresses* (Grand Rapids: Eerdmans, 1965), 1–2.

6. As quoted in Jack Canfield and Mark Victor Hansen, *A Second Helping of Chicken Soup for the Soul* (Deerfield Beach, Fla.: Health Communications, 1995), 13.

7. N. H. Muller, "The Christmas I Loaned My Son," in Jack Canfield et. al., *Chicken Soup for the Christian Soul* (Deerfield Beach, Fla.: Health Communications, 1997), 43–44.

8. Bernard Rimland, "The Altruism Paradox," *Psychological Reports* 51 (1982): 521, quoted in Martin Bobgan and Diedre Bobgan, *How to Counsel from Scripture* (Chicago: Moody, 1985), 123.

9. Dee M. Taylor, "A Special Gift," in Jack Canfield, Mark Victor Hansen, and Barry Spilchuk, *A Cup of Chicken Soup for the Soul* (Deerfield Beach, Fla: 1996), 136–37.

10. "Suicide, Accident, or Homicide?" *Journal of the Academy of Forensic Scientists,* 14 August 1998, as cited on the Internet at: http://www.inter-nexus.net/~ashahsov/funnies/suicide.net.

11. C. S. Lewis, *Weight of Glory,* rev. ed. (New York: Macmillan, 1980), 1.

12. Eddie Ogan, "The Rich Family in Our Church," 20 August 1998 as cited on the Internet at www.gotelltheworld.com/illustrate/rich.htm. This web site contains hundreds of indexed illustrations.

13. C. S. Lewis, *Mere Christianity* (New York: Macmillan, 1952), 116.

14. Quoted in J. Allan Peterson, *The Myth of the Greener Grass* (Wheaton, Ill.: Tyndale, 1992) as cited in James S. Hewett, ed., "Revenge of Love," *Parables, Etc.,* August 1993, [disk, Saratoga Press, Plateville, Colo.]. Available through The Autoillustrator, P.O. Box 5056, Greeley, CO 80631.

15. Paul Brand with Philip Yancey, "And God Created Pain," *Christianity Today,* 10 January 1994, 18–23.

Chapter Six

BARRIERS

TO LOVE

$\mathcal{N}$ot long ago a New York City landlady was ordered by a judge to face some of the practical effects of disregarding the Golden Rule. Newspapers around the country reported that Florence Nyemitei, age seventy-one, had been ignoring the judge's orders to clean up the apartment building she owned. When her tenants had complained that they lacked hot water, heat, and other necessities, Judge JoAnn Friia ordered her to pay a fine of five thousand dollars and to place an additional fifteen thousand in an escrow account to be used to repair her building.

But Nyemitei did neither. Things eventually became so bad in her building that residents had to rig a string of Christmas lights from a nearby building in order to illuminate the hallways. (She hadn't paid the power bill.)

In response, Judge Friia ordered Nyemitei to spend four nights a week in her own building over a period of several months. The landlady complained about the verdict, saying, "It's not fair to put me in prison at this time of my life." One resident of her apartment building had a different view of things:"At least she'll have to suffer like the rest of us."[1]

Nyemitei had, in effect, created a prison for the people around her to live in. A lot of us are like that. That's not necessarily our intention, but that's the impact of our actions. But beware: The environment we create for others has a way of capturing us in its grip as well. A Christian who wants to obey God's command found in the Golden Rule must constantly ask himself, "Am I creating a hospitable or a hostile environment for the people around me?"

I remember a clever comic strip some years ago in which a little boy expressed his intention to become a physician when he grew up. One of his siblings predicted that he would never make it because he didn't love mankind, to which the aspiring doctor replied, "I do so love mankind; it's just people I can't stand."

Those who would love others as themselves may find that loving mankind in theory can be rather different from loving people in reality. If you expect a trouble-free experience in obeying the Golden Rule, you are setting yourself up for some surprises.

Although a number of those surprises are unavoidable, you can avoid stepping on many a land mine by abstaining from practices that weaken or damage personal relationships. Three common barriers to loving others are unrestrained anger, careless speech, and the fear of failure.

EXPRESSIONS OF ANGER

RULING OUR INNER SPIRITS

The first barrier is not simply "anger"; it's our *expression* of anger. The initial rush of emotion when someone displeases us is not necessarily sinful by itself. Anger is OK (see Ephesians 4:26). It becomes sinful when we lose a grip on ourselves and do or say hurtful things in response. God's Word insists that the one who would obey the Golden Rule must in the process learn to rule his own spirit. The classic expression of this principle comes in Proverbs 16:32, "He who is slow to anger is better than the mighty, and he who rules his spirit than he who takes a city." When you read something like that, you tend to think of it as a pardonable bit of poetic license. It is not. For every person who rules his spirit, there are a dozen military leaders who can conquer a city.

Failure to rule the spirit is as old as human history. It has been exhibited by people who displayed amazing competence in other areas. For example, Alexander the Great justified his title from a military point of view, but as a human being he often showed that he was a stranger to ruling himself. Once, Alexander attended a banquet with some of his generals to celebrate a recent conquest. One general in attendance, named Clitus, was a capable leader who had served Alexander for years. He had also been on the military staff of Alexander's father, Philip of Macedon. Unfortunately, he had too much to drink at the celebration and began to chide Alexander's grandiose lifestyle compared with his father Philip's simplicity.

Alexander flew into a rage and went after Clitus. Friends separated the two, and Clitus was escorted from the room for his own safety. Foolishly, however, he later returned, unseen, through a different door. He then stood behind some tapestries and began to quote a Greek poet who had composed an ode that was critical of Alexander. The enraged ruler quickly grabbed a nearby spear and threw it at the curtain, mortally wounding his lifelong friend.

Alexander was horrified at what he had done. He rushed to the fallen Clitus and pulled out the spear, turned it around, and tried to fall on it himself, but was restrained by his officers. For days afterward, he raved about his terrible action; but the harm was irreversible. He knew how to conquer cities, but not his own rages.

The measure of your greatness is seen in what it takes to get you upset. The person with discretion, or good judgment, overlooks a great deal. Proverbs insists, "The discretion of a man makes him slow to anger, and it is to his glory to overlook a transgression" (19:11). Internal restraint shows a person's glory; lack of it, his shame.

THE EXAMPLE OF CHRIST

The greatest of all examples of such glory, of course, is the Lord Jesus Himself. Can you imagine the number of ridiculous things that were said and done in the presence of Him who was Truth itself? Things like: "Lord, it is good for us to be here; if You wish, let us make here three tabernacles: one for You, one for Moses, and one for Elijah" (Matthew 17:4). That was the only time in history that a human being, the disciple Peter, was told from heaven to keep quiet. God's voice was heard on the mountain, saying, "This is My beloved Son . . . Hear *Him!*" (Matthew 17:5, italics added). The Lord Jesus listened patiently for years to a considerable amount of empty and irrelevant jabbering. His greatness, in part, was measured by the things He overlooked. When you endure hurts without retaliating, you are imitating Him.

Foolish people, by contrast, are quick to take offense,

ready to see an insult in the tiniest gesture. Haman decided to wipe out all the Jews in Persia because one man, Mordecai, refused to bow down to him (Esther 3:1–6). Haman's anger should have been reserved for something more substantial.

HOW OUTBURSTS WOUND RELATIONSHIPS

Bonds patiently constructed over months and years by loving others can be cut in an instant by an outburst of temper. Consequently, if you take the Golden Rule seriously you will learn to avoid harboring hostile attitudes —the sort that make us determined to get what we want regardless of who is hurt.

I read not long ago of a pastor who left his ministry after only a few years. He entered medical school and eventually became a physician. When a friend wanted to know why he would make such a change, he responded, "I discovered while in the ministry that people will pay more to take care of their bodies than their souls."

After some years as a doctor, he abandoned his medical practice to attend law school and become an attorney. Again his friend wanted to know why. He explained, "I found out that people will pay more to get their own way than to care for either body or soul."[2] Those who are willing to pay that kind of price will find that it is incompatible with loving others as themselves.

CARELESS SPEECH

Outbursts of anger create great difficulties for the believer who wants to obey the Golden Rule, but we don't have to display uncontrolled anger to cause problems. We only have to be careless with our tongues.

Did you ever hear of the Boxer Rebellion? No, it was not an uprising of professional pugilists who were unhappy with their share of ticket revenues. It was much more serious than that. The Boxer Rebellion took place in China a century ago. Provoked by a group known as the Society of the Harmonious Fists—or more simply, the Boxers—the common people took part in an outburst of antiforeign violence that left hundreds of people brutally murdered. Along with large numbers of Chinese Christians, 188 foreign missionaries and their children died, often in horrible ways.[3]

Many factors contributed to the emergence of the Boxers, but the trigger for the outburst of violence came through some careless, erroneous talk. It began in 1899 when reporters from four Denver papers needed a story —any story—for the Sunday editions. The four happened to meet on a Saturday evening in the Denver train station. They were there in hopes of spotting a visiting dignitary whom they could pump for information; however, nobody important came into Denver that day.

The four walked to a nearby hotel to have a drink together. As the slow news evening wore on, one of the antsy reporters announced that he was going to invent a story and turn it in. The others thought that might be a good idea. Why not pool their efforts and come up with a real barn burner of a story they could all use? Having it appear in all four papers would add validity.

A local or statewide story would be too easy to check on, so they decided to write an item describing events in another country. China seemed a good possibility. One of them had an idea: The Chinese government has decided to demolish the Great Wall. They have already put the job up for bids, and several American firms are bidding on it.

Objections were considered. Why would the Chinese destroy such a national symbol? "Simple," someone said; "they want to show the world that they are interested in foreign trade and promoting international goodwill."

The four reporters explored their invented story from all the angles. Finally, the details were finished, and they were satisfied. To give credence to the whole shady business, they moved to another hotel and registered under fictitious names, passing themselves off as New Yorkers coming through town. They put out the word that they had just been interviewed by local reporters about an important foreign project and would be leaving town in the morning.

On Sunday, all four Denver papers carried the story on their front pages. One headline read: "Great Chinese Wall Doomed! Peking Seeks World Trade!" Newspapers from the eastern seaboard picked up the story; eventually it worked its way into the foreign press.

When the information began to appear in Asian papers, ordinary Chinese citizens were disturbed at the thought of Americans coming to destroy a national treasure. The Boxers took advantage of this seething resentment and whipped their countrymen into a frenzy, resulting in hundreds of deaths and the invasion of China by troops from six countries to protect their nationals.[4] Were the Boxers responsible for the chaos? Directly, yes, but remember that the upheaval began only after four lazy newspapermen decided to spread a rumor. And rumors—false information given to defame or injure someone—are one form of careless speech.

Thoughtless or critical speech pours acid into relationships. Placing a bridle on the tongue will minimize its damage, but learning to replace unkind words with golden ones is better. Kind speech will build significant relationships. The apostle Paul did not simply say, "Let no corrupt communication proceed out of your mouth"; he added, "but what is good for necessary edification, that it may impart grace to the hearers" (Ephesians 4:29).

Corrupt words have a way of being issued in response to an attack, but Proverbs gives sound counsel about how to speak: "A soft answer turns away wrath, but a harsh word stirs up anger" (15:1). Andrew Jackson won the Battle of New Orleans in part because he stacked cotton bales to take the brunt of the British artillery shells. The shells exploded well enough, but their energy was dissipated in blowing cotton fiber into the air.

People are not persuaded by angry words but by gentle ones. Anger may raise a righteous cause in our hearts, but gentle speech will transfer it to the hearts of others: "By long forbearance a ruler is persuaded, a gentle tongue breaks a bone" (Proverbs 25:15).

The word of God is very clear. Christians are never to be content simply to speak the truth. Paul said that we must speak the truth in love (Ephesians 4:15). Speaking the truth is crucial, but speaking the truth in love is the only valid form of Christian communication.

FEAR OF FAILURE

For most Christians, anger and careless speech are problems they understand. Fear, however, can form a hidden reef when putting the Golden Rule to work. It keeps us from taking steps to love others because we are afraid we might be misunderstood or unappreciated.

A lot of us are like the farmer who was sitting on his porch on a beautiful day in July. A stranger came along and asked, "How's your cotton coming?"

"Ain't got any," he explained. "Didn't plant none. 'Fraid of the boll weevil."

"Well, how's your corn?"

"Didn't plant none. 'Fraid o' drought."

"How about your potatoes?"

"Ain't got none. Scairt o' tater bugs."

The visitor finally asked, "Well, what did you plant?"

"Nothing," the farmer answered. "I just played it safe."[5]

You can't play it safe and obey the Golden Rule. Count on it: If you try to love people, you will, sooner or later, be misunderstood or unappreciated (or both)—at least at first. But you have to love them anyway.

TAKING THE EXTRA STEP

During the smaller early worship service in one church, the visitor wasn't difficult to spot. She was fashionably dressed and exuded an air of independence. Mrs. Chandler estimated that the visitor was about the right age for her Sunday school class, so when the service ended, she invited her to attend. The newcomer declined politely but firmly.

The following Tuesday, Mrs. Chandler discovered by calling the church office that the cool visitor had turned in a guest's card. After obtaining the phone number from the church secretary, she called the lady and thanked her for coming to church. The response was a distant "Thank you for calling."

The woman did not return the following Sunday, so Mrs. Chandler and another woman from the class went by and knocked on the visitor's door. She did not invite them in. They were disappointed but decided that they could at least pray for her.

Several weeks later, acting on an impulse, Mrs. Chandler stopped by and knocked on the door. This time the reception was not cool. "I guess you just don't get it, do you? I don't want to go to your church, I don't want to come to your women's Sunday school class, and I have had it with you bothering me all the time. Please don't call me or come see me again. Ever!"

Mrs. Chandler was dismayed and hurt, but she resolved to pray for the woman and did so almost every day. Months passed. Then one fateful evening the phone rang. It was Mrs. Chandler's pastor explaining how the woman's husband had been killed in an accident, and the pastor said, "She asked if I would call you and let you know."

Mrs. Chandler drove to the house and rang the bell. The young woman opened the door. Throwing her arms around Mrs. Chandler's neck, she sobbed, "I knew you'd come."[6]

Many people would never have been in that position. They would have given up at the first rebuff, fearing a second rejection. However, the Golden Rule commands us to focus on others and their welfare. The moment we begin to wonder what they think of us, we lose the gilt edge on our relationships with them.

The solution is to find your own security in the abundant love that God has already demonstrated toward you. "God demonstrates His own love toward us, in that while we were still sinners, Christ died for us" (Romans 5:8). The security provided by that proven love ought to encourage you to take a few risks in His interests. Take the extra step to help others. And do not fear their potential rebuffs.

A few years ago, I visited Westminster Abbey in London. In this magnificent building are housed the graves and memorial markers of many of Britain's greatest people. One marker is in memory of Lord Stringer Lawrence, a brilliant military man, famous for being the founder of the Indian army. His accomplishments as a general were staggering, and he was held in awe by his contemporaries. His memorial plaque at the Abbey says simply: "He feared man so little because he feared God so much." We need more of his ilk in the Christian church today—people who are unafraid of the spiritual challenges posed by loving others.

CHASING FEAR BY FINDING COURAGE THROUGH CHRIST

Fear, at the root, comes from looking at our future and realizing that our resources are inadequate. Jesus, however, said in John 16:33, "Be of good cheer; I have overcome the world." He didn't say, "Be of good cheer; you have overcome the world." Taking risks requires keeping in touch with the great Overcomer. When Jesus repeatedly told the disciples, "Fear not," He was not inhibiting their emotions. He was telling them to have courage to overcome their emotions. Courage cannot exist except in the presence of fear. If you are never afraid, you will never need courage, because courage, by definition, is strength for the overcoming of fear.

Fear becomes a problem when it provides a roadblock to doing what is right or doing what is wise. When you have a friend who doesn't know Christ, and you are afraid to inquire about the state of his soul because you may be rejected, fear has caused you to do wrong. Find your courage through Christ, who commands us to take courage in what He has accomplished for us.

You will stay away from people who may be spiritually needy if you give in to your fears. If you avoid people because you are fearful that you might commit a social faux pas, you are yielding to the Enemy on this point. Take it from one who has committed a thousand social blunders, the fear is worse than the reality. I have made every mistake in the social rule book and a few that Miss Manners never dreamed of. But you cannot build friendships and you cannot love people biblically if you let your fears keep you away from them.

Dwight Eisenhower is the only U.S. president to have publicly professed his faith in Christ and been baptized while in office. He was a highly decorated soldier, and as president he could have called for great pomp and ceremony, but the baptismal service was simple and unpretentious. Heads of state and leaders from all over the world were present. The services were televised internationally.

The president was not reluctant to bear testimony even among the great. When Soviet Premier Nikita Khrushchev toured the United States in 1959, he spent a weekend at Camp David with the president, during which the two leaders had several private chats. One Sunday morning during the state visit, the president invited Khrushchev to accompany him to church. When the Soviet leader declined, the president attended alone.

Years later, when Eisenhower died, Khrushchev sent a telegram of condolence to Mrs. Eisenhower, which included the words, "He (Eisenhower) was the only man in America who inquired about my soul." In view of the persistent rumors that Premier Khrushchev professed faith in Christ before his death, this incident may be even more important than it seems. It never would have happened if the president had let his fears of rejection keep him from reaching out to a man who was reputed to be harsh and unforgiving.

OBEYING THE GOLDEN RULE:
THE GREAT ADVENTURE

Obedience to the Golden Rule by its very nature is an adventure. It calls for the best that we have, because we walk in the steps of Christ when we look out for the needs of others. It helps to ask ourselves, "Where would I be if Christ had not taken great risks to bring me to Himself?" It also helps to remember that that same Lord has overcome death and has promised to be with those who make Him known. The Golden Rule forms a challenge to take part in a process that will stretch us and give Him opportunity to make His goodness and faithfulness known to us and to others. Once we know how much we can count on Him, reaching out to others becomes easier.

One of the most effective advertisements ever written appeared in a London newspaper early in the twentieth century. It read, "Men wanted for hazardous journey. Small wages, bitter cold, long months of complete darkness, constant danger, safe return doubtful. Honor and recognition in case of success." Not exactly appealing copy, to be sure. Yet thousands of men responded, because it was signed by Sir Ernest Shackleton, noted explorer of the South Pole. Recalling the many letters, Shackleton said, "It seemed as though all the men in Great Britain were determined to accompany us."[7]

The course of the expedition certainly justified Shackleton's cautious recruiting approach. In December 1914, he and the twenty-seven men he chose from among the thousands of applicants left the whaling station on South Georgia Island near the tip of South America and headed toward Antarctica. The ship *Endurance* in which they were embarked was scarcely out of sight of land when things began to go wrong. The wind came up, the seas became agitated, and vast blocks of floating ice began to appear.

It wasn't long before the ice closed in, and the ship couldn't move. Despite the skillful application of both sails and engine, they were held fast. For ten months, in fact, they could not move, and finally the *Endurance* was crushed by the pressure of the expanding ice floes.

The explorers had seen this coming and prepared for it. They unloaded the food they had stored for their expedition, along with the lifeboats and their tents and other necessities, onto a huge ice floe. The ice was their home for five months as they drifted in the swelling waters through the Antarctic winter.

Fifteen months after departing, they were finally able to launch the lifeboats, and after a week at sea they landed on an uninhabited rock known as Elephant Island. There Shackleton left the twenty-two of his men who were too weak to travel. He and the other five set out for their original port at South Georgia Island, some eight hundred miles away.

After a perilous journey, suffering from the cold and the huge waves that threatened to swamp them at any moment, they landed on South Georgia, wrecking their lifeboat in the process. Too late they realized they were on the wrong side of the island. The whaling station was thirty miles away across a range of glacier-filled mountains.

Shackleton and two of his men left the other three behind, crossed the mountains, and found the help they needed. He explained the desperate situation and was able to return for the men left on the leeward side of the island. Next, Shackleton immediately borrowed a vessel and began attempts to return for the twenty-two men still on Elephant Island. Weather and ice forced him to turn back on his first attempt. On a second try, he and his companions made it to within twenty miles of the island, but again he had to turn back. A third try also failed.

Acutely conscious of his men's desperate situation, he borrowed still another ship and set out for Elephant Island. What he couldn't know was just how terrible their conditions were. For five months, the men on Elephant Island had somehow managed to exist on a narrow extension of sand at the base of an ice-covered cliff. They had constructed a makeshift hut by combining boulders, packed snow, and the two lifeboats. They had subsisted on seal and penguin meat with melted snow for their water.

Yet they managed because they believed in Ernest Shackleton. They trusted in his promise that he would look out for them. Shackleton had left a man named Frank Wild in charge. Frank's optimism helped keep them focused. Every day for five months, he would rise, roll up his sleeping bag, and say, "Get your things ready, boys, the boss may come back today." Sure enough, one day the mist parted and there was Shackleton returning to get them.[8]

As sure as Frank Wild trusted in Shackleton's commitment to them, we can trust in Jesus' care for us. He who loves us invites us to follow Him. He bids us become lovers of others for His sake. The risks are great, but the Master is greater, and the rewards are eternal. Don't let your fears keep you from the adventure.

NOTES

1. "Landlady Sentenced," *Seattle Times,* 18 January 1998. As found on Internet edition of the newspaper. Available at www.seattletimes.com/news/nation-world.

2. S. I. McMillen, *None of These Diseases* (Old Tappan, N.J.: Revell, 1963), 75–76.

3. James and Marti Hefley, *By Their Blood* (Grand Rapids: Baker, 1979), 9–44.

4. Adapted from Paul Aurandt, *More of Paul Harvey's The Rest of the Story* (New York: Bantam, 1981), 136–38.

5. James S. Hewett, ed., *Illustrations Unlimited* (Wheaton: Tyndale, 1988), 204–205.

6. "I Knew You'd Come," in Jon Allen, ed., *Illustration Digest,* January–February 1992, 5–6.

7. Warren W. Weirsbe, *Be Faithful* (Wheaton, Ill.: Victor, 1981), 13.

8. Arthur Maxwell, "Hoping Against Hope," *Review and Herald,* in Jon Allen, ed., *Illustration Digest,* September–November 1993, 1–2.

Chapter Seven

THE VALUE

OF SERVANTHOOD

*R*ay Stedman, late pastor of Peninsula Bible Church in Palo Alto, California, used to love to tell the story of how he once asked a boy in the church what he wanted to be when he grew up. The young man's answer was, "A returned missionary."

The youthful observer was perceptive beyond his years. He had been around long enough to know that missionaries who have come home after years of faithful ministry abroad receive much honor. He figured he would like to receive the congratulations and do the celebrating without the necessary preliminaries of actual service.

The Golden Rule requires, however, that we follow in the steps of the Lord Jesus by submitting to His gentle yoke of serving people. Such a notion sometimes goes down hard—at least until we understand how it is supposed to work.

Jesus' disciples James and John once requested that they be placed at His right and left hand in the future kingdom. The Lord Jesus then told them the proper method of being considered for such high honors: "Whoever desires to become great among you shall be your servant" (Mark 10:43). Today we read these words after their corners have been worn smooth, but at the time, they must have stung.

THE MYTHOLOGY OF SERVANTHOOD

Today, Jesus' proposition inviting believers to become servants sounds almost trite. We have heard His words so often that they resemble a platitude, one of those lukewarm, squishy statements that nobody wants to challenge but no one wants to obey either. But this call to serve is anything but commonplace. It contains a formula so powerful that it will revolutionize your life if you pay attention to it.

Unfortunately, we often entertain ready-made myths about servanthood that keep us from taking it too seriously. Let's consider three.

"I Will Be Trampled Upon"

First, we think servanthood means being trampled on by others. It does not. The Lord Jesus did not permit people to trample on Him—not out of pride, but because He knew the Father's purposes would not be advanced that way. He knew that genuine servanthood is not a passive activity. Jesus was often direct and assertive. He drove the money changers from the temple at least twice. He insisted that His Word was right even when He was publicly opposed by the religious authorities. He stood up in public and condemned the hypocrisy and immorality so common in the clergy.

Thus, servanthood does not mean that you are to lie down and let others walk on you, nor does it mean that you jettison all of life's true pleasures. When Jesus submitted to the Crucifixion, He did not yield passively to the will of others; He actively chose to do what would benefit others. Jesus, "taking the form of a servant . . . humbled Himself and became obedient to the point of death" (Philippians 2:7-8). He insisted that He was going to the Cross to offer His life voluntarily in response to God's will: "No one takes it from Me, but I lay it down of Myself. I have power to lay it down, and I have power to take it again. This command I have received from My Father" (John 10:18).

Servanthood means voluntarily engaging in the tasks that are often less than glamorous but which benefit others. The Christian who imitates a doormat helps no one. Servanthood is not unselfishness, which is a fundamentally negative concept; it is the embodiment of love, which is positive.

That is why the Lord Jesus repeatedly told His disciples in advance that He was going to be arrested and crucified. Shortly after Peter's great confession of Jesus as the Messiah, the Lord entrusted the disciples with a shocking secret. His future was to go to a cross: "He began to teach them that the Son of Man must suffer many things, and be rejected by the elders and chief priests and scribes, and be killed, and after three days rise again" (Mark 8:31).

They needed to know that what was about to happen to Him was not simply a trick of fate. Crucifixion was in the divine plans. Jesus submitted to cruelty because in doing so He gained the ability to cure the disease that caused the cruelty. People gained by His loss, but in the end He gained too.

Being crucified was not weakly yielding to what He couldn't control. It was a forthright assertion of His commitment to complete His mission as a servant. Servanthood requires that one behave in a similar manner often. Servants don't always wait to be asked to serve; they seek out needs to which they can respond and take the initiative by getting involved, even if it means serving uncooperative people.

James Dobson likes to tell the story of William Slonecker, a physician and friend. Dr. Slonecker, a pediatrician, examined many children, but one patient was a particularly obnoxious ten-year-old, Robert, the terror of the doctor's office. Robert would attack the whole clinic when he came for a checkup. He would grab instruments and files and telephones and generally make destruction into an art form. Meanwhile, his passive mother would just shake her head in bewilderment.

During one physical examination/tantrum, Dr. Slonecker observed several cavities in Robert's teeth and concluded that he would need to be referred to a local dentist. But on whom do you bestow such a dubious honor? The chances were good that the dentist who treated Robert would also no longer accept referrals from Dr. Slonecker. At any rate, the doctor finally found an older dentist with the reputation of knowing how to deal with troublesome children. He prepared him as best he could, and the fateful day came when Robert showed up, ready as always for battle.

The dentist said, "Get in the chair, young man."

"No chance," was the reply.

"Son, I told you to climb onto the chair, and that's what I intend for you to do."

"If you make me get in that chair, I will take off all my clothes."

The dentist paused a minute, and finally said, "OK, son, take 'em off." Robert immediately removed his shirt, undershirt, shoes, and socks. Then he looked defiantly at the dentist, who said, "All right. Now get on the chair."

"You didn't hear me," Robert said. "I said if you make me get in that chair, I will take off *all* my clothes."

The dentist again told the boy, "Son, take them off." So Robert did, becoming a pinkish imitation of the proverbial jaybird.

The dentist said, "All right, into the chair." Fresh out of options, Robert did as he was told and sat cooperatively throughout the entire procedure. When his cavities were repaired, he was told he could get out of the chair.

Robert said, "Give me my clothes now."

The dentist said, "I'm sorry, Robert, but you can tell your mother that we're going to keep your clothes overnight. She can pick them up in the morning." So Robert walked with his mom out through the crowded waiting room, past the startled and snickering onlookers, into the hall, down the elevator, and out into the parking lot.[1]

The next day, his mother returned to get his clothes and told the dentist: "You don't know how much I appreciate what happened here yesterday. You see, Robert has been blackmailing me about his clothes for years. Whenever we are in a public place, such as a grocery store, he makes these unreasonable demands, and if I don't give in, he starts his routine about taking off his clothes. You are the first person who ever called his bluff. The impact on him even overnight has been incredible."[2]

In serving others, you will meet the belligerent and the unappreciative. The dentist served him, helping the boy have better teeth; he endured the boy's threats and resisted his demands. Servanthood doesn't mean that you must agree to conform to the stated wishes of those you serve. Robert's mother had been agreeing to his demands for years, but it was his dentist who served him.

People also object to the idea of being a servant for other reasons.

"I WILL HELP OTHERS AND RECEIVE NOTHING IN RETURN"

Sometimes we reject the call to service for another reason: We think servanthood benefits everybody but us. Jesus, however, taught that servanthood leads to future greatness. Servanthood doesn't just change your character right now; it reserves for you rewards of immeasurable worth.

James and John are often criticized for approaching Jesus as they did in Mark 10:37: "They said to Him, 'Grant us that we may sit, one on Your right hand and the other on Your left, in Your glory.'" I heard one preacher call this "a shameful ambition." It is nothing of the sort. What greater compliment could you pay the Lord Jesus than to want to be near Him throughout the age to come? Greatness in the kingdom is a noble ambition.

What is not noble is that the brothers had only a shallow perception of what such high honors require. Jesus immediately pointed out that being honored with Him requires a willingness to suffer along with Him. He said, "You do not know what you ask. Can you drink the cup that I drink, and be baptized with the baptism that I am baptized with?" (Mark 10:38). The cup and the baptism are figurative ways of referring to His suffering and death. He drank the bitter cup of separation from the Father. At Calvary, He was immersed in sufferings so terrible that humanity can scarcely conceive of them. Were James and John willing to undergo such harsh treatment for a place next to Him in the kingdom?

Servanthood is the key to a rich position in the kingdom, but it also benefits the servant in other ways. For example, servanthood gives the servant a present sense of fulfillment and well-being—and may even improve his health. Several programs have been developed in recent years involving seniors. In one national program involving large local hospitals, volunteers serve as foster grandparents on pediatric wards for the benefit of young patients facing prolonged hospitalization. Many of the suffering youngsters they visit have working parents who can rarely come to see them. Some of the young patients come from great distances and even foreign countries. In such cases visits are practically impossible, so these young people face a lonely hospital bed without anyone nearby who is important to them. The effect of this loneliness and monotony, as you might imagine, is terrible. Many children sink into an uncommunicative depression and even refuse to eat.

Enter the "foster grandparents." In this program, to become a foster grandparent, people must meet certain qualifications. For example, they have to be over sixty and living on a limited income; they must be willing to devote at least twenty hours a week to the work. In exchange, the foster grandparent receives a small weekly income, free lunches in the hospital cafeteria, and free transportation to and from the hospital. Many of the foster grandparents also have significant health problems, but these don't prevent them from building affectionate relationships with their needy "grandchildren."

The results have been wonderful. The children look forward to the grandparents' visits—being read to, played with, having company at mealtime, or even being fed by the grandparents. The children spring back from their sadness and begin to respond well to therapy.

Several of these programs have discovered additionally that the foster grandparents enjoy great improvements in their own health. Their blood pressure comes down, their sleep improves, and their energy increases as they spend time at their "grandchild's" bedside. They find joy in a renewed purpose for living at a time when they badly need it. In serving others, their own lives are made rich.[3]

So servanthood really does benefit the servant, both in the age to come and right now. But serving others for Christ's sake also changes the people we serve. It argues strongly against another commonly held myth about servanthood.

"I Won't Accomplish Much."

Servanthood doesn't accomplish anything, some skeptics say. Certainly, servanthood isn't the world's path to greatness, but it is Christ's. Real servants always make a difference. Take, for example, the experience of those prisoners of war in the Kwai River Valley of Burma during World War II. Hollywood produced an Academy Award–winning film years ago called *The Bridge over the River Kwai*, but, as so often happens, they missed the real story.

In his book *Through the Valley of the Kwai*, Ernest Gordon included the spiritual dimensions of the events. He described the remarkable life and death of a Scotsman by the name of Angus McGillivray. Angus and the other prisoners (Americans, Australians, and British) were transported to Burma to build the now famous bridge.

Conditions were brutal. The cruelties of the Japanese guards were, perhaps, to be expected. What was surprising, according to Gordon, was the hostility among the prisoners themselves. Most of them had lost hope of surviving the war, and as a result they had settled into the habit of living for the moment. Prisoners typically stole from each other. Men would sleep on their belongings and still items would disappear from beneath them. Everyone was out for himself—right up until the day they heard Angus McGillivray had died.

At first, nobody believed it. He was such a huge person that it didn't seem possible that camp conditions could do him in. As it turned out, they didn't. Angus died taking care of his "mucker."

Gordon explains that the Scots' regiments maintained a buddy system in the camp; a man's buddy was called his "mucker." It was every man's responsibility to make sure his mucker survived, and Angus's mucker was very ill. In fact, everybody had given him up as a lost cause —except for Angus.

Somebody stole the mucker's blanket, so Angus gave him his own. Camp rations were below subsistence levels, so Angus gave his buddy his own food. Through this gentle giant's servanthood, his dying friend began to make a remarkable recovery. Unfortunately, the effort was more than Angus himself could handle, and one day he collapsed and died.

When the news of his sacrificial actions began to filter through the camp, things started changing. The prisoners became ashamed of their previous behavior and began to think of ways to encourage each other. Camp members crafted musical instruments and started a small orchestra. Somebody found a New Testament and decided to begin a Bible study. Ernest Gordon was not a Christian, but he was a university graduate, so he was asked to take charge of the study.

As these desperate men read the New Testament, God's truth broke through. Gordon and others became Christians, and the changes in their lives and attitudes were so profound that more people began to attend the meetings—including even some of the Japanese guards. From the study sprang a hospital, a humble lending library, and even a university of sorts—all because of one man who exhibited the heart of a servant.[4]

God made us to be servants. In fact, it is not extreme to say that we are servants by creation, looking for a suitable master to follow. If we don't find the right one, we end up serving ourselves and being terminally bored. Far better to come to Christ, The Servant, and discover that in serving Him we become truly free—and experience the joys of serving as well.

THE OPPORTUNITIES FOR SERVANTS

IN CHURCH MINISTRY

With those three myths attacking our minds, no wonder we hesitate to serve. In fact, the number one problem in churches across America today is probably a shortage of servants. Religious journals are full of references to how difficult it is to recruit people to do the work of ministry. Every church I know of has this problem. Yet throughout the New Testament, and especially in the Golden Rule, it's clear that to describe oneself as a Christian is to make a claim of servanthood. For those who become servants, joy awaits.

Christian servants are in short supply. Typically, about 20 percent of the people in the local church do about 90 percent of the ministry that is overtly church connected. We have a saying in church ministry: "He who is faithful in a little shall be swamped with much!" One has to make jokes about it to keep from weeping.

This regrettable situation is caused in part by the reality that a lot of church ministry offers little immediate recognition. Those are the jobs that often go begging. People forget the truth behind myth two: In serving, there are rewards, both now and in the future. One of those is the joy of helping others. If you're willing to serve, you won't have to ask twice. The need is great, but the reward is lasting.

One woman in my own church was convinced she could never teach Sunday school. With a great deal of reluctance, she accepted a one-quarter commitment to teach fifth and sixth graders. When she saw the excitement on those bright faces, however, and saw how God could use her to shape young lives spiritually, she never had to be asked again. She found, as have many others, that happiness comes from doing what God put us here to do.

IN LENDING

There are also many ways to engage in loving service outside the walls of a church building. A church auditorium is a sacred place to most of us, but we need to remember the familiar story of the lady who showed up as a visitor in a small congregation. Everyone was sitting in silence. "When does the service begin?" she asked a man sitting near her. His answer: "As soon as the meeting is over."

Those are words fitly spoken, for most of the meaningful application of the Golden Rule takes place outside the traditional hours of church ministry. We love our neighbors, usually, in places other than the confines of a church building: in our homes, neighborhoods, schools, and businesses.

One of the golden ways to reach out to others is to offer them the use of your possessions: ladders, pickup trucks, leaf blowers, or whatever is needed. Even better, offer them some assistance in their current project. One person who understood servanthood noticed that his neighbor was having trouble with a riding lawn mower. So, he grabbed a handful of tools and walked over to lend a hand. In just a few minutes, the mower was working again. The mower owner, admiring his friend's toolbox, asked, "Say, what do you make with such a fine kit of tools?"

The answer was perceptive: "Mostly friends."[5]

THROUGH HOSPITALITY

You can open your home to people and show them kindness for Christ's sake. You don't have to do anything fancy; just invite them over for a bowl of ice cream. College students and military people often miss the warmth of home when they are away. You will find your own heart gladdened as you provide them a place to enjoy good food, company, and conversation.

Bill and Helen Furnish were high school sweethearts

who married soon after their graduation. They had to work hard to make ends meet as they put themselves through college as a married couple. After college, Bill found a good job as a salesman and they decided that they could begin a family. Time passed, however, and no child came. They waited for eleven years. Their strong Christian faith was tested as they waited for God to bring a baby into their lives.

In 1951, it finally happened, and they were overjoyed. They named their little son Steven, and they showed him great love, especially since the doctor told Helen that bearing additional children would pose a significant health risk to her.

Their happiness was complete as they watched Steven grow up and become a fine young man. After he graduated from high school, he and some of his friends decided to join the Marine Corps. Shortly after completing his training, Steven was shipped to Vietnam.

He was killed by a sniper's bullet on his first patrol.

The Furnishes were devastated. For several months, Bill took a leave from his work and they mourned for Steven. The company then offered Bill a transfer to southern California. He accepted in the hopes that the change of scene would help Helen and him deal with their grief.

The Furnishes settled in Oceanside, a pleasant seacoast community north of San Diego. They had not been long in their new home before they realized they were living only a short distance from Camp Pendleton, a large Marine Corps base. They were surrounded by young people in uniform, each one a stinging reminder of Steven. They wondered why God had seemingly placed them in an area where their wounds were being ripped open again and again.

After church one Sunday they stopped for lunch at a small restaurant with an ocean view. For a time they discussed how to make sense of their situation. On the way home, they saw a young marine hitchhiking with a sign that read, "Home." On an impulse, Bill stopped the car and offered the young man a ride.

The marine explained that he had just finished basic training and was headed for Arizona to see his parents before being shipped overseas. Bill took the young man to the local bus station and bought him a ticket to Arizona, explaining, "You can waste a lot of valuable time hitching a ride. I know your folks must be anxious to see you."

Finding their own spirits lifted through the experience, Bill and Helen made a commitment to God to be available to those young marines God would send their way as they lived in Oceanside. Their pastor encouraged them to begin a hospitality ministry to the young trainees, which they did, enlisting many others from their church as well.

Several of the women in the church began a "cookie ministry" to provide home-baked treats for marine recruits. Bill had business cards printed with the Furnishes' name and address and the phrase, "A Home Away from Home." As dozens of young people passed through their lives, their own pain was eased, and they experienced a strong sense that God had indeed brought them to Oceanside to do good for themselves and for others.

One day they received a letter that read:

Dear Mr. and Mrs. Furnish:

You probably don't remember me, but I was hitchhiking a few weeks ago and you picked me up. I just had to write and tell you something. When you picked me up, I had run away from the base. I was AWOL. I was angry and confused. I felt that no one in the world cared whether I lived or died. But you were so caring to me. You were so kind. Mr. Furnish, when you prayed with me and slipped me that twenty dollar bill, I tried to be cool, but Mrs. Furnish, when you hugged me and told me you hoped to see me again, my heart broke. I did not know of another person on earth who wanted to see me. I cried when the bus pulled away.

When you picked me up, I had decided that if a car picked me up, I would kill the people and steal the car. I had a sharpened bayonet with me, and as soon as I got into your back seat I took it out of my bag and laid it on my knees. But as we drove along in the car, you talked kindly to me and showed me love. Your spirit was so sweet that I just could not do as I had planned. If you'll look under the back seat of your car, you'll find where I hid the knife when you weren't looking.

Bill and Helen looked, and there it was. The Furnishes eventually hung that bayonet on the wall of their den, very close to the picture of their son Steven and the dozens of photos of young marines to whom they have ministered. Their conclusion: "Tragedy can make you bitter or better. It all depends on whether you hold it inside or give it to God. We're just glad we can be part of His work here on earth."[6]

Christian servants know that God's purpose for their lives is fulfilled as they love others through serving them. We don't have to be greatly skilled, but if we take what we do have and serve others with it, we will know the joys that come through identifying with the One who did not come to be served, but to serve.

NOTES

1. Adapted from James Dobson, *Dr. Dobson Answers Your Questions* (Wheaton, Ill.: Tyndale, 1982), 109–10.
2. Dobson, *Dr. Dobson Answers,* 110.
3. Edith Sarah Stein, *A Time for Every Purpose: Life Stories of Foster Grandparents.* Book available from Knowledge, Ideas and Trends, 11131-0 Tolland Turnpike, Suite 175, Manchester, Conn. 06040 or on the Internet at www. booktrends.com/book12.htm.
4. Ernest Gordon, *Through the Valley of the Kwai* (New York: Harper & Row, 1962), as quoted in Tim Hansel, *Holy Sweat* (Waco, Tex.: Word, 1987), 146–47.
5. Michael P. Green, ed., *Illustrations for Biblical Preaching* (Grand Rapids: Baker, 1989), 158.
6. "A True Story," in Jon Allen, ed., *Illustration Digest,* April–June 1989, 1–2.

Chapter Eight

LOVING

THE UNLOVELY

*D*uring the days following the American Revolution ... ed in Ephrata, Pennsylvania, a Baptist
... Miller. Pastor Miller had long been a
... shington, then serving as the first
... delphia, some seventy miles from
... Ephrata, Miller had to deal with
... was anything but a friend.

... mself by doing all he could to
... able, and he took a particular
in ... er Miller's life. Among other
am... ved to spread slanderous stories
abo... and at least once physically attacked and
injured the preacher.

Wittman also extended his hostile activities beyond
his hometown. Eventually, his sinful escapades caught up
with him, and he was arrested for treason. He was tried
and sentenced to death. Pastor Miller easily could have
applauded this development, but he refused to do so.

Instead, he walked seventy miles to visit his longtime friend, George Washington, and to appeal for a pardon for Michael Wittman. When he arrived, the president expressed delight in seeing his old friend once again.

"Well, Peter, it is a pleasure to see you. What can I do for you?"

"I have come to beg for the life of the traitor Wittman," replied Miller. "I know that you won't refuse me."

Washington brought him up short: "I cannot do this. This case is too black. I am sorry I cannot give you the life of your friend."

"My friend!" exclaimed the old preacher. "He's the bitterest enemy I have." Miller then related some of his dealings with Wittman.

"That puts another light on the matter," said the president. "I could not very well grant you a favor by giving you the life of a friend. But I will give you freely a pardon for your enemy." Peter Miller then took Michael Wittman back home to Ephrata, but not as an enemy.[1]

THE POWER TO TRANSFORM

Miller understood the principle that Abraham Lincoln later expounded. When northern radicals insisted near the end of the Civil War that the South should be severely punished for its rebellion, since they were "enemies," Lincoln resisted, and explained his own approach by asking, "Do we not destroy our enemies by making them our friends?"

This is the call of every follower of Christ. We are to love our enemies, to pray for those who persecute and abuse us. (See Matthew 5:44–48.) Lincoln was right:

Loving people is the most direct route to transforming enemies into friends. Such unconditional love possesses the power to transform people.

The godly always have enemies. While we ought to try to make them our friends, we may not always be able to do so. However, even when that transformation doesn't happen, Scripture extends a hopeful principle: "When a man's ways please the Lord, He makes even his enemies to be at peace with him" (Proverbs 16:7).

The existence of enemies often confuses those with godly intentions. We can understand how people could despise or resent us before we came to know Christ; but surely now, after our conversion, after we have at last begun to make some progress in Christian growth, we have eradicated (we hope) most of the reasons why they should detest us—yet they continue to do so.

In wrestling with this phenomenon, Christians easily forget that the Lord Jesus had enemies—many enemies. Much of His ministry was spent dodging magistrates and religious leaders who wanted to throttle Him: "After these things Jesus walked in Galilee; for He did not want to walk in Judea, because the Jews sought to kill Him" (John 7:1). Even worse, a man who was a close associate and in whom the Lord had invested a great deal eventually would betray Him. No servant, seeking to obey the Master's Golden Rule, has a right to expect exemption from such experiences. Nor can we fail to love those who think little of us.

FAMILY CHALLENGES

Loving the unloving begins at home. Whether it's an unforgiving in-law or a wayward uncle, we will encounter family members who irritate us, offend us, or reject us. As servants, we must demonstrate love to *all* our family.

One of the most challenging opportunities God ever gave me to love the unlovely came in the person of my mother-in-law. When Cheryl and I began to talk seriously of marriage about six months before I graduated from college, both her parents supported our plans. I was the captain of the UCLA basketball team at the time, and pro scouts were following my college career with a modest degree of interest. If the NBA didn't offer an opportunity, I already had the promise of a job with a major defense contractor, so the future looked promising. My relationship with Vi, Cheryl's mom, was excellent at the time. I admired her as a person with an infectious sense of humor and as a mother deeply devoted to her daughter—a trait I fully understood.

Several months before the wedding, the Lord began to create a desire in my heart to serve Him in some type of preaching ministry. I endured some tense moments during this process, because when I had proposed to Cheryl I had no plans to spend a life in vocational ministry. Now we were engaged, and I felt newly inclined to head in a different direction. Pro ball seemed like a dull option; so did the defense job. I knew it wasn't fair to presume that she was ready to become a preacher's wife. We talked about it at length, however, and she made it clear that she was with me wherever God might lead us together.

We hoped that her parents, regular churchgoers, would be excited as well, but it was not to be. Norm, Cheryl's dad, was ambivalent; even worse, Vi thought my plans to attend seminary foretold doom for her little girl. She was convinced that Cheryl and I would end up in some remote jungle where her daughter would wash clothes on the riverbank and her grandbabies (if they survived) would grow up with crocodiles for playmates. While that wasn't exactly the scenario I had in mind, I had to confess to her that I couldn't really be sure what kind of ministry I would be drawn to—or where we would settle.

Vi was so upset with the turn of events she could hardly talk to me—and for years after we left California didn't talk to me except when she could not avoid doing so. She did, however, talk to Cheryl. The content of the conversation sometimes included references to the meanness of her son-in-law in taking her only child off to Texas to seminary—and who knew where after that.

After seminary, we came to Atlanta, even further from Vi's southern California home. Over the next few years, Cheryl and I turned our attention to beginning a family and a new church and tried to return kindness for Vi's hostility; but it was never easy. Though often invited, she visited our home only twice, when each of her first two grandchildren were born. Her coldness to me was a source of grief to Cheryl and to Norm, who had by this time adjusted to our situation. (Norm came to see us— by himself—at least once a year.)

Apart from these visits, the only conversations we had were those I initiated on the phone (usually on holidays, anniversaries, and birthdays). While her reluctance to talk and barely veiled hostility proved taxing, I felt strongly that I had to make the effort. Just because she held a grudge against me was no reason for me to behave the same way and shut her out in return. Cheryl and I prayed for her often, but we saw little change in her for eighteen long years.

Unexpected hardships eventually eroded the little island Vi had built for herself. Shortly after Norm returned home after a Christmas visit to us, he lost his eyesight during the course of a single day. Doctors called it a vascular accident involving the blood supply to his optic nerves. In the morning, he could see. By dinnertime, he was totally and irreversibly blind.

Caring for Norm over the next few years drained Vi's physical resources. We offered repeatedly to move them to Georgia so that we could assist in caring for him, but she would have none of it. Finally, we received a call from a caring neighbor who described just how ill Vi had become in the last couple of months. (Nobody knew it at the time, but she had tuberculosis.) Cheryl and I called, and again I offered to fly to California, help sell the house, and move them across the country to be with us. There was obvious relief in Vi's voice as she accepted the offer.

She was so ill that she only lived three months after the move, but it was a period Cheryl and I will never forget. The realization that I was committed to caring for her and Norm finally broke through. She confessed that her stubborn resentments had cost her dearly through the years. "I don't know what happened," she said. "The devil somehow got his hooks into me." She again became cheerful, funny, and affectionate with me and the whole family, right up to the day the Lord took her home. Had I failed to behave consistently in those difficult years, we might never have known the joy of seeing her freed from the hostility she carried around for so long.

I tell that story in the hopes that it will encourage you, yet I know that it contains the potential to mislead too. Not every effort at loving difficult people will have a positive ending. Some people will challenge you right into their graves (or yours). We don't love people in the hopes of a happy ending. We love them because it's the right thing to do. And remember, loving the unlovely includes everyone from a close family member, to a distant relative, to the obnoxious neighbor living next door.

OF EGOISTS AND NARCISSISTS

It is easy to forget that God didn't wait to love us until we were lovable. "When we were enemies we were reconciled to God through the death of His Son" (Romans 5:10). We are supposed to imitate His actions rather than yield to our own inclinations.

Love those who offend and expose you, even as Jesus did. We must extend the Golden Rule to our enemies.

Years ago I heard a lecture by an Englishman attempting to describe the mind-set of the Western world. If we are to express Christ's love effectively, this pastor argued, we must understand the current mental climate. People in the Western world, he explained, think in terms that are fundamentally narcissistic rather than egoistic. An egoist owns a strong fixation on himself and his own interests. He cares little what people think. He is simply out for himself and is utterly indifferent to others. (The central characters in the Ayn Rand novels are egoists, for example.) A narcissist, by contrast, focuses on himself by looking around to see what everybody else thinks of him. Unlike the egoist, he has no strength of character. He is fundamentally insecure.

For that reason, a narcissist is exceptionally sensitive to the opinions of others. The moment others show any lack of sensitivity to him (for example, by telling an ethnic joke), he comes apart because he has no basis for holding any opinion of himself except what others tell him. (It is certainly no accident that the slang verb *diss*, a shortened form of *show disrespect*, has come into use in these days.)

"JESUS LOVES ME, THIS I KNOW"

Because you and I—indeed most Americans—are part of the present narcissistic environment, that selfish attitude is likely to affect our efforts to love others as ourselves. Christians should both live distinctively and love distinctively in this environment. You and I should live distinctively by forming opinions of our own value not from the expressions of others but from unalterable biblical facts.

The key fact is this: God sent Christ into the world to die for us. That never would have happened if He had not loved us; and whatever God's love touches, it makes valuable. We will find peace and assurance as we recall the simple yet profound truth of the children's song: "Jesus loves me, this I know, for the Bible tells me so."

The Christian should also love distinctively by loving unshakably. Today even the most sacred forms of love seem tenuous. People form and drop attachments with astonishing quickness. Christians ought to shine brightly against such a dark background as we demonstrate our commitment to Jesus Christ by our commitments to others. We ought to find our greatest security in God's love. If we do, loving the unlovely won't be easy, but it will be possible.

DEALING HONORABLY WITH DIFFICULT PEOPLE

The apostle Paul appointed his friend Titus to what had to be one of the ancient world's most challenging ministries. Titus was to be Paul's representative to the church on the island of Crete in the Mediterranean. He was to try to repair a wounded church in a place where a native had described his countrymen as "liars, evil beasts, lazy gluttons" (Titus 1:12). To make matters worse, the Roman authorities on the island looked at Christianity through hostile eyes. What counsel do you give a man who must work in such uninviting conditions? How do you love Cretans?

COOPERATION

Paul told Titus that if he attempted to live in an environment with difficult people, the first thing to remember was not to be difficult himself. The watchword in dealing with unbelieving people in the world is *cooperation*. Paul told Titus to instruct the local Christians "to be subject to rulers and authorities, to obey, to be ready for every good work" (Titus 3:1).

Roman magistrates were not known for their restraint in dealing with Christians at the time of Titus's ministry. It was during the days of Paul and Titus that Roman emperors first began to arrest believers and torture them. Some eventually tied Christians to tall posts in their gardens, had them covered with pitch, and set them ablaze to serve as torches during garden parties.

If cooperation is the byword of honorable dealings with difficult people who are non-Christians, then one natural temptation would be to submit and then to seek some kind of retaliation with the tongue. Not so, said Paul:"Speak evil of no one, be peaceable, gentle, showing all humility to all men" (Titus 3:2). It takes far more power to be unretaliative, peaceable, gentle, and humble toward difficult people than it does to lash out in misguided retribution toward them. Only a work of God in the heart can enable us to love people that way.

A HUMBLE HEART

The humble heart and gentle spirit can exist anywhere—even in the dark of prison and misfortune. In *The Church in China,* Carl Lawrence tells about a young Christian who was arrested and beaten by the authorities because of her faith. Only nineteen years old, the Chinese woman was roughly thrown into a dungeon after the beating. The underground cell was utterly dark and the floor was wet. The odor of human excrement was overpowering. The tiny bedless room seemed to have an overpopulation of rats and insects.

As she took stock of her miserable surroundings, she felt liquid dripping down her arm. She realized that she was bleeding as a result of her mistreatment by her captors. And all she could do was sit on the floor amid the foul conditions and hope that her wounds wouldn't become infected.

Or was that all?

She decided that she would not give in to her surroundings. She began in the manner of the apostles by thanking the Lord that she had been considered worthy to suffer for Him. She asked God for wisdom and strength—not to be able to leave the prison, but that she might be able to bring spiritual light to her dark new home.

As she reflected in the following days, she wondered to whom she could minister. Suddenly it came to her. She stood and called for the guard. "Sir, can I do some hard labor for you?"

The guard was astonished. He hadn't heard that one before.

"Look!" she said, "this prison is so dirty, there is human waste everywhere. Let me go into the cells and clean up this filthy place. All you will have to do is give me some water and a brush."

After some hesitation, the guard left, returning with the materials she had requested. She began to go from cell to cell, cleaning away layers of encrusted filth—and in the process whispering the gospel of Christ to others. Some of them had suffered far worse than she had and had long ago given up all hope of having meaningful contact with another person. Her evangelistic efforts met with immediate success. After just a few weeks, nearly all the prisoners had become Christians.

Her ministry, however, landed her in trouble with the communist prison officials. They discovered that their tortures no longer held the terror they once did for prison inmates. Those hopeless creatures could even look their captors in the eye and say, "We forgive you in the name of Jesus."

Talk about honorable dealings with difficult people!

After the young woman received one beating herself, the warden gave her paper and a pencil and told her to write out a confession of her sins against the state. "Lord," she prayed, "I have done nothing wrong. What shall I write?" She decided to write out her testimony.

After the warden read it, he called her into his office and began to scream at her. He decided to humiliate her by reading her antirevolutionary drivel before the other prison officials. Soon they were all sitting around the room, listening to the reading of the testimony of this Christian teen. The warden began to read the words more slowly as he progressed. It was apparent that he (and probably some of the other officials) were being deeply affected by the words of this young woman, who lived out among difficult people the apostolic pattern of gentle cooperation given to Titus.[2] The ripples from her prison-bound testimony are still being felt in the region.

RECALLING OUR MOTIVE

But if cooperation and humility are the manner of our dealings with authorities, what may be even more important is our motive in dealing with difficult people. The why of what we do is just as important as the what. And the "why" has to do with remembering what our lives were like before Christ. Paul reminds us: "For we ourselves were also once foolish, disobedient, deceived, serving various lusts and pleasures, living in malice and envy, hateful and hating one another" (Titus 3:3). It is easy to forget that every Christian was once a non-Christian. Once we have begun to grow spiritually, we tend to forget our unredeemed beginnings, and that can turn us into harsh people. We need to consciously call to mind what we were like as unbelievers. We need to extend to others the same grace that someone gave to us.

A good memory will help in that process. In Deuteronomy, God gave instructions that once a year every worshiper should go up to the temple in Jerusalem and take part in a prescribed ritual. The worshiper was to take some of the produce of his fields and bring it to the priest at the altar. He was to say to the priest, "I declare today to the Lord your God that I have come to the country which the Lord swore to our fathers to give us." Then the priest was to take the basket out of his hand and set it down before the altar and the worshiper was to continue: "My father was a Syrian, about to perish, and he went down to Egypt and sojourned there, few in number; and there he became a nation, great, mighty, and populous" (Deuteronomy 26:3–5).

Why would God prescribe a ritual like that? Because He knew that when people reach the "great, mighty, and populous" stage they tend to forget that they were not always that way and to chalk their advantages up to their own superiority. God wants us to remember that He deserves the credit for whatever we are.

SHOWING GOD'S KINDNESS

God brought us out of a mess akin to Egyptian slavery. According to Titus 3:4, our rescue began with God's kindness. "But when the kindness and the love of God our Savior toward man appeared." If kindness moved us out of our difficulties, perhaps kindness will move somebody else out of his. In dealing with difficult people, it is wise to remember this: Kindness and humility seem like small things, but small things can change people's lives permanently.

During the Civil War, a group of soldiers were carrying on a friendly conversation. One of them remarked that he had learned to be especially careful about small things. "Would you believe," he said, "that a little thing like a pair of socks changed the entire course of my life?"

"I can hardly believe that," replied his companion.

"Well, it's true! Once I planned to take a trip with some of my friends on a canal boat, but two days before we intended to leave, I injured my foot while chopping wood. It was only a small cut, but the blue dye in the homemade socks I wore poisoned the wound, and I was compelled to stay at home. While my friends were on their journey, a preacher came to our town to hold gospel meetings. Since I didn't have anything else to do, I decided to attend. The message touched me deeply, and as a result, I surrendered my heart to the Lord Jesus Christ. Afterward I saw that I needed to change my life in many ways. New desires and purposes took hold of me. I determined also to seek an education, for I trusted that this would enable me to live more usefully for my Lord." The person who made these comments? James A. Garfield, a man who eventually became president of the United States. [3]

God uses the little things in men's eyes—things like kindness and humility, the basic working capital of a servant—to accomplish great things for Himself.

LOVING DIFFICULT PEOPLE IN THE CHURCH

If loving difficult people in the world is tough, loving them in the church is in some ways more of a challenge. You expect to find harsh and demanding people in the world, but not in the sacred company of believers. Yet several portions of the New Testament were written to help people like Timothy and Titus deal with unruly church members.

BE SURE YOUR PRIORITIES ARE RIGHT

If that is where you find yourself in your attempts to live out the Golden Rule—facing disobedient or divisive believers each Sunday—start by making sure your own priorities are in order. Paul said, "This is a faithful saying, and these things I want you to affirm constantly, that those who have believed in God should be careful to maintain good works. These things are good and profitable to men" (Titus 3:8). Good works become important once a person has believed. Good deeds have nothing whatever to do with becoming a Christian.

Actually, I take that back. Good works do have something to do with becoming a Christian. They form a barrier to it. Good works can become actions that people rely on instead of relying on Christ to save them—and relying on anything that is empty yields no help. According to a United Press International story, a catastrophe was averted several years ago in a Midwest city when a hospital official discovered that firefighting equipment installed when the building was constructed had never been connected. For thirty-five years, the equipment had been relied upon for the safety of the patients in case of emergency, but it had never been attached to the city's water main.[4]

The medical staff and the patients had felt complete confidence in the system. They thought that if a blaze broke out, they could depend on a nearby hose to extinguish it. But theirs was a false security. The costly equipment lacked the most important thing—water. The hospital staff was trusting in emptiness. People often make the same mistake when it comes to their eternal destiny. Good works are an empty hose when it comes to becoming a Christian.

On the other hand, good works have everything to do with being a Christian. Titus says to "affirm constantly" (Titus 3:8) that those who have believed in God should be careful to maintain good works. Good works are the fruit of spiritual life, not the root, and good works form the tangible expression of the Golden Rule in most cases.

AVOID USELESS ARGUMENTS

We first make sure our own priorities are in order, and then determine to stay away from useless arguments. "Avoid foolish disputes, genealogies, contentions, and strivings about the law; for they are unprofitable and useless" (Titus 3:9). Debating how many angels can dance on the head of a pin doesn't justify the breath it takes to do it. Tracing your genealogy back to show you came from an important line is trivial. Take heed of the subject matter before you start (or continue) an argument.

However, church leaders like Titus sometimes have to do more. They must stop an argument that has already broken out—for the sake of the peace of the church. In Titus 3:10–11, Paul's direction is very clear: "Reject a divisive man after the first and second admonition, knowing that such a person is warped and sinning, being self-condemned." There are people in every church, Paul said, who seem to exist just for the heartaches they cause. When Titus finds someone who delights in setting one part of the church against another, he should warn him once. If he persists, warn him again. After that, reject him. Don't take anything he says seriously. Arguments with such people are a waste of time. No sincere Christian is interested in stirring up hostility.

The apostle goes further in helping Titus's understanding. According to Paul, any person who lives to create divisions has three serious internal problems:

- He is warped—his values are off base.
- He is sinning in ways that may not be visible to the church at large.
- His secret sins have resulted in a wounded conscience, coloring the way he looks at events and people.

FOCUS ON JESUS

In contrast to being occupied with such unprofitable people, Paul urged Titus to "send Zenas the lawyer and Apollos on their journey with haste, that they may lack nothing. And let our people also learn to maintain good works, to meet urgent needs, that they may not be unfruitful" (Titus 3:13–14). Problems with difficult people in the church will be largely avoided if people will keep their eyes where they belong.

Focus on Jesus. Focus on accomplishing His mission of spreading the good news of salvation. Just as people like Zenas and Apollos were supported on their missionary trips, believers must focus on meeting *urgent* needs. When the church is busy getting God's work done, it will not have time for power trips.

Loving the unlovely may be one of the greatest spiritual challenges, but Jesus Christ mastered the process.

Those who are His cannot escape such a holy responsibility.

NOTES

1. Leslie B. Flynn, *Come Alive with Illustrations* (Grand Rapids: Baker, 1988), 144.
2. Carl Lawrence, *The Church in China* (Minneapolis: Bethany, 1985), 43–45.
3. Cited in "Historical Anecdotes," *Fresh Sermon Illustrations* (online). Available on the Worldwide Web at http://fp.sedona.net/budman/archives/970310.html .
4. Adapted from the account in "No Water," *Bible Illustrator,* computer disk. Available by subscription from Parson Technology, 1700 Progress Drive, Hiawatha, IA 52233.

Chapter Nine

THE GOLDEN
MINISTRY OF PRAYER

The lights of Rochester, New York, twinkled against the dark landscape below. We had been due to land there at ten o'clock, but here it was nearly half past, and the plane was still circling.

It was one of those moments when my imagination began to make me uneasy. Finally, after what seemed an interminable delay, the captain announced that our airplane was experiencing a mechanical problem. The possibility existed that the plane's nose gear might collapse on landing. (He didn't need to tell us what would happen after that.) The pilot continued by explaining that air traffic control had cleared all traffic below us. He would attempt the gentlest possible landing, allowing the nose gear to touch down only after our landing speed was as slow as he could safely make it.

Then he made two unsettling requests: Would passengers please be sure their seat belts were fastened, and when we came near the ground, lean forward in their seats?

The passenger cabin suddenly became quiet. You didn't have to be a preacher to realize that a lot of people had recently become interested in prayer. I smiled to myself as I remembered an old story. A minister traveling on an international flight heard the pilot announce that the plane was in danger. Almost immediately, the preacher's seatmate began to scream. Then she remembered that she was sitting next to a minister, grabbed him by the shoulder, and began to shake him, shouting, "You're a preacher. Do something religious!" So he took an offering.

I had no time to take an offering; I was too busy praying.

As you can tell by the fact that you are reading this, we landed safely. The touchdown was as soft as a mother's kiss, and when we ended our landing roll the passengers released a heartfelt outburst of grateful applause. I hope that a lot of them remembered to thank God as well. I certainly did.

People tend to be somewhat schizophrenic about prayer. When we are in danger, we can be quite earnest about it. When it comes to the day-to-day routine, however, we have trouble stifling yawns. We often have to be dangled over a precipice before we see how important prayer can be to us. But prayer's impact is generally acknowledged even by secular agencies.

Several years ago, newspapers reported that Superior Court Judge William Constagney of Charlotte, North Carolina, began each session of court by bowing his head and engaging in silent prayer. But five lawyers and the North Carolina branch of the American Civil Liberties Union (ACLU) demanded that the judge cease and desist from his praying.

Judge Constagney explained that he was simply trying to set the tone for a proper atmosphere in the courtroom. His opponents argued that it is illegal to use religion to control the judicial atmosphere.

As I read the newspaper account, I wondered: Does the ACLU admit that prayer can actually affect what goes on in a courtroom? For Christian believers, the answer is obvious, as is the application of prayer to personal relationships. In prayer we learn dependence on Him, as well as sensitivity to the needs of others and a conciliatory and humble spirit. That will go a long way toward applying His balm to hurting people.

Yet most people do not pray regularly. Some time ago, *Newsweek* magazine ran a feature with the title, "Can Modern Man Pray?" The conclusion of the article was that most could not.[1] Unfortunately, prayer is not just a snag for the general population—a great many Christians struggle with it as well. What is more, people are reluctant to admit that their prayer lives are not what they would like. So each Christian goes about thinking, *I must be the only believer dissatisfied with his prayer experience,* an altogether invalid conclusion.

HOW PRAYER FULFILLS THE GOLDEN RULE

God gave us prayer for more than moments of danger. He wants us to join Him in accomplishing His work in the world, and prayer is one of His appointed means of doing that. Praying for people forms a key part of obedience to the Golden Rule. To be convinced of that, just ask yourself: Do I want others praying for me and my needs?

Even beyond the good things that happen to those

for whom you intercede, several internal changes take place in yourself when you pray for people. Those changes prepare you to have a stronger commitment to love others and thus fulfill the Golden Rule.

AN INCREASED ATTACHMENT TO PEOPLE

The first inner change that occurs is *when praying for others your interest in them increases.* William Law once said, "There is nothing that makes us love a man so much as prayer for him." It is nearly impossible to pray consistently for people and to dislike them for very long. (You can manage, but you have to work at it.) By an invisible law of the soul, we tend to be drawn to those we pray for. That is true whether we intercede for an individual or even for whole countries.

Bob accepted Christ as his Savior after the witness of his friend Doug. As part of discipling his new brother in Christ, Doug introduced Bob to the ministry of prayer in an unusual way. Learning that Bob had an interest in a particular country in central Africa, Doug issued a challenge. He asked Bob to pray for that country every day for a month. If nothing important happened there to advance the cause of Christ during that time, Doug would pay Bob five hundred dollars. (He obviously knew something that Bob didn't.) The only requirement was that Bob would pray *every day.*

Nearly a month went by, and not much was happening. Right before the month was up, Bob attended a dinner where he happened to meet a woman from "his" country. He immediately began to ask questions. Where did she live? What kind of work did she do there?

The woman worked in a medical center. Encouraged by his obvious interest, she invited him to fly to Africa and look in on the work she and her colleagues were doing. He did so. He discovered, among other things, that the center's pharmacy shelves were practically empty. He knew he could do something about that.

Returning home, Bob began to make phone calls to contacts at various pharmaceutical houses, telling them of the critical shortage of drugs where he had been. He collected more than one million dollars worth of donated medicine and sent it to the African medical center.

The recipients appreciated his kindness so much that they invited him back—and paid for his airfare this time. During the second visit, the president of the country came by to express his thanks and to give Bob a tour of the country's government center. In the process, Bob noticed some prisoners and asked about them. The president explained that they were political prisoners, people who disagreed with the president's approach to governing the country. Bob expressed his regret that the president had found it necessary to lock them up; it didn't seem like a good idea to imprison people on account of their opinions.

Shortly after Bob returned to the United States, he received a call from the State Department. They asked if he had said anything to the president of that country about his political prisoners.

"Sure," Bob said, "I told him I thought it wasn't a good idea."

The State Department representative then informed Bob that the prisoners had been released shortly after his visit. State had been working to free them through diplomatic means for a long time, but nothing had worked.[2]

God works, however, in places where diplomats have no power at all; and results came when one man made a commitment to pray for people in a distant land for one month.

An Increased Confidence in God

Not only does prayer change our level of involvement with people we pray for, *it gives us an increasing amount of confidence in God.* As we see Him answer prayer repeatedly, it makes it easier to lay our next request before Him. That's important, because loving people as ourselves can be a tall order. We need to know God can make us equal to the challenge, and to know that God is able to effect big changes in people—even people who seem to be hard and unresponsive.

When I was in seminary in the late sixties, I remember hearing one of my favorite professors, Howard Hendricks, tell the story of his dad. Dr. Hendricks' parents had been divorced when he was small, and he had lived with his mother during his formative years. Though he loved and admired his dad, he was concerned about his father's spiritual condition.

By the time I studied under him, Hendricks had been praying for his father for more than thirty years, but his dad had never shown any interest in the gospel. It was only after I had graduated that I read the rest of the story in one of his books.

Howard's father, George Hendricks, was a military man and was stationed in the Washington, D.C., area during some of his years in the army. He was a self-reliant individual who had proven his toughness on battlefields around the world. His family's periodic attempts at engaging him spiritually seemed to bounce off him with little effect. So they kept praying.

While they were interceding, God was working—but in ways they couldn't see. Butch Hardman, an independent Bible church pastor in Arlington, Virginia, not far from the Pentagon, had begun listening to Dr. Hendricks on tape. He heard Howard refer to his father, and it reminded him of his own dad and his spiritual needs. Butch attended a Philadelphia seminar at which Dr. Hendricks spoke and introduced himself. He also began to pray for George Hendricks.

Then one day Butch was driving the church bus. He had just dropped off his passengers when he saw a man standing on the street corner who bore a striking resemblance to Howard Hendricks. I'll let Howard tell what happened next:

> [Butch] backed up the bus, stopped, got off, and went over to the man.
>
> "Are you by any chance Howard Hendricks' father?"
>
> It is easy to imagine the startled response. "Er ... ah ... (I can envision my father's critical once-over with his steely blue eyes) yeah—you a student of my son?"
>
> "No, I'm not, but he sure has helped me. Got time for a cup of coffee?"
>
> That encounter began a friendship, skillfully engineered by the Spirit of God. Butch undoubtedly sensed dad's hesitancy when he discovered he had met a preacher. For a long time Butch did not invite him to attend his church. He simply suggested that dad drop by the office for coffee. Patiently he endured dad's cigars and his endless repertoire of war stories. Before long he also learned

that dad had been diagnosed as having a terminal throat cancer.

Months later Butch was at his bedside. "Mr. Hendricks, I'll be leaving shortly for a Holy Land trip. Instead of my listening to you tonight, would you let me tell you a story?"

Butch had earned his hearing and he began simply to relate the interview of Jesus Christ with Nicodemus as recorded by the Apostle John. At the conclusion dad accepted Butch's invitation to receive Jesus Christ as his own personal Savior. Then dad got up out of bed, stood, and saluted with a smile. "Now I'm under a new Commander-in-Chief!"...

The last time I saw dad alive I could not believe he was the same man I had known. His frame was wasted, but his spirit was more virile than I had ever known.

In accordance with dad's specific provision in his will, Butch Hardman conducted the crisp military funeral in Arlington Cemetery where the gospel of Jesus Christ was presented to the small group of family and military attendants. As the guns saluted their final farewell, I knew God had vindicated forty-two years of prayer.[3]

If we pray, God will soften hearts and open avenues of ministry to the most resistant of people.

NEW OPPORTUNITIES FOR SPIRITUAL CONVERSATIONS

If we take one more step in addition to praying, *God can use it mightily to open doors for spiritual conversations.* That additional step is to *offer to pray* for people. I have asked through the years, "Is there anything I can pray about for you?" I have yet to have anyone refuse to take the question seriously. Even people with a reputation for skepticism appreciate it when you take that kind of interest in them. The recipients of your concern may not want to open up at the moment you ask about them, but at least you are on record with them.

I don't necessarily recommend the approach, but Mordecai Ham, noted evangelist of the early twentieth century, used prayer as an unorthodox evangelistic tool. When he went to a new community, Ham would refuse to sit and talk with Christians between meetings. He always wanted to be taken to the most outspoken sinners in the community.

Ham's fame sometimes preceded him, and on one occasion a farmer with an immoral reputation, a professing atheist, hid in a cornfield when he heard that the evangelist was nearby. Ham found him, nonetheless, whereupon the man asked what his intentions were. Mordecai said that he was going to pray for the man— specifically, he was going to pray that God would kill him. When the farmer protested, Ham told him he shouldn't be disturbed by the idea. Wasn't he an atheist? Did he not profess that God didn't exist? How could he fear what a nonexistent God might do in response to prayer from a deluded believer?

On the other hand, Ham said, if there was a God, didn't death seem an appropriate punishment for a man who had poisoned the spiritual prospects of so many? The atheist pleaded with him not to pray for his death. Ham instead prayed, as was his intention all along, for the man's salvation. At the evangelist's final meeting in the community, Ham baptized the man and his family as new converts.[4]

While in India a few years ago, I asked a local pastor what he did to gain credibility with the Hindu population that dominates that large country. He replied that he waited until a significant problem arose in someone's household, then knocked on the door and offered to pray for that person. Whether it was connected with the answers he received or merely his display of compassion, his prayer ministry proved to be an effective evangelistic tool.

Prayer may be one of the most effective ways we can minister to people, as the Indian pastor and the southern evangelist discovered. It will open spiritual doors like little else.

THE LOVE CONNECTION

An effective prayer life is connected to a love of people, for how we pray depends on who we are. Jesus said, "Therefore I say to you, whatever things you ask when you pray, believe that you receive them, and you will have them" (Mark 11:24). Some read that statement and all they see is the condition that is attached: "Believe that you receive them." So they "try" as hard as they can to believe. Prayer becomes a kind of self-hypnosis; we tell ourselves, *if I can just talk myself into believing hard enough, God will have to do what I want.*

But the important thing about Mark 11:24 is not the attached condition. The critical issue is the people to whom it was addressed. Jesus said those words to the small group of people who knew Him best in the whole world, and who would know Him even better soon afterward. They were words spoken to people with a commitment not only to know Him, but to make Him known. He was entrusting them with great privileges in prayer and exhibiting a principle that we dare not miss.

Here's an analogy. Let's say that I suddenly come into possession of ten million dollars. After all my bills are paid, I decide to spend the remaining money with people who are dear to me. To these people I make a proposal: "I want to spend ten million dollars where it will do some real good, and I want you to share in the joy of this experience. I have reserved a million dollars just for you. Where do you want to spend it? You say the word and I'll write the checks."

I could do that in confidence, because those people I choose are dear to me—they know me—*and they would want to spend the money the same way I would.* I would not issue an invitation like that to many people—only those who could be trusted with it.

That's an argument for becoming a person who is close to the Savior. If we share His purposes, we will find that prayer will become a delight rather than a problem. And our prayers will be effective.

When we pray for people, we engage in the same cause that God is engaged in. We show our concern for what is eternally valuable in His mind. We do for others what we delight in having done for ourselves.

NOTES

1. "Can Modern Man Pray?" *Newsweek*, 30 December 1968, 38–39.
2. Raymond McHenry, "Motivational Stories," a collection of illustrations on computer disk, 78. Available from the Christian Communicator's Research Service, 6130 Barrington, Beaumont, TX 77706.
3. Howard and Jeanne Hendricks, *Footprints* (Portland, Ore.: Multnomah, 1981), 17–19.
4. Raymond McHenry, "Motivational Stories," 276.

Chapter Ten

BUILDING BRIDGES

OF FORGIVENESS

C.C. McCabe, a one-time Civil War chaplain, served God with distinction in the ministry of the Methodist Episcopal Church in the late nineteenth century. McCabe was an active church planter, an effective evangelist, and a peerless missions fund-raiser.

Once while traveling by train in California, McCabe noticed a young man sitting near him who seemed nervous and out of sorts. When the preacher inquired about the young man's restlessness, the latter explained that he had just been released from prison and was headed home. His nervousness grew from not knowing whether his parents would welcome him back. To make things less embarrassing for them, he had written them a letter explaining how they could let him know if he would be welcome at home after his release. He wrote, "If it is okay to stop by the house for a visit, just tie a rag in the old tree by the back porch." He knew he would be able to see the tree from the train as he passed by the family farm. "If there is no cloth in the tree, I'll just keep on going," his letter had said.

As the train neared the farm, the young man found the tension too great and asked McCabe if he would look and let him know whether there was a white cloth hanging from the tree. The train rounded a turn, giving McCabe a clear view of the farm. Leaping to his feet, he shouted at the young man, "Look! Look!"

The tree was covered with white rags.[1]

For years afterward, McCabe told the story as an example of God's approach to forgiveness. God's generous and merciful heart lies at the basis of eternal forgiveness, and His Word provides instruction on how Christians are to forgive others. Part of obedience to the Golden Rule is knowing how to respond once you have behaved in an unloving way (or someone else has). Such knowledge is made essential because close relationships often dissolve because people don't know how to be reconciled.

In a fallen world, offenses and the marred relationships they produce have a way of multiplying. In Spain, they tell the story of a father and son who became alienated. The son left home because of what he felt was mistreatment by his father. Grieving, the father set off to find him and searched for months with no result. Down to only a few options in his quest, the father placed an ad in a Madrid newspaper that read: "Dear Paco, meet me in front of this newspaper office at noon on Saturday. All is forgiven. I love you. Your Father." On Saturday, eight hundred Pacos showed up.[2]

Many people in the world carry around terrible pains connected with unresolved offenses, particularly within their own families. If you have not experienced such alienation, time may well change things. Sooner or later you may offend someone you love—or you will be offended by such a person. The breach must be repaired biblically, or the relationship will suffer or even end. God wrote the Book on how to maintain good relationships —and how to mend broken ones. People who desire to obey the Golden Rule must know how to receive forgiveness and how to extend it.

WHAT TO DO WHEN YOU WOUND OTHERS

Jesus insisted that people who wound others must go to the wounded person and ask for forgiveness. Reconciliation even takes precedence over worship: "Therefore if you bring your gift to the altar, and there remember that your brother has something against you, leave your gift there before the altar, and go your way. First be reconciled to your brother, and then come and offer your gift" (Matthew 5:23–24). Even God is willing to wait while Christians take the necessary steps to repair broken relationships.

It does not matter who is more responsible for the offense. A Christian cannot say to himself, "Joe is guiltier than I am in this matter; he ought to call me first." Guilt percentages are irrelevant. If you remember that your brother has something—anything at all—against you, go. If he remembers anything that he has done to offend you, he should go. In an ideal world, Christians would meet each other halfway, each proceeding to ask for forgiveness from the other. And Christians would not wait for a nonbeliever to say "I'm sorry"; instead the believers would approach first.

WHAT TO DO WHEN WOUNDED

But what if *you* have been offended and no one is asking you to forgive him or her for the offense? What do you do then? If you said, "I go to the offender and point out the offense," you are close, but not quite on target. It may come to that, but that's not where you start. How do you behave lovingly toward a person who has offended you?

Most of the time, you simply overlook the offense. The vast majority of sins that are committed against us are comparatively minor in nature. They may irritate, but they are not catastrophic. They don't keep us awake at night, and most of the time the offender is unaware he has done or said anything to hurt us.

The biblical sage gave the principle for dealing with offenses of this sort: "The discretion of a man makes him slow to anger, and it is to his glory to overlook a transgression" (Proverbs 19:11). Overlooking transgressions is the way we make room in our world for other people to live in it. Christians should not become hypersensitive worrywarts who make an issue out of every slight.

King Solomon expressed it another way: "Hatred stirs up strife, but love covers all sins" (Proverbs 10:12). Covering the dismaying actions of others toward you with love is simply making allowances for the fact that they may not be where God wants them to be spiritually right now ... and the chances are good that they exercise a similar restraint toward you just as often.

WHAT TO DO WHEN
A HURT CAN'T BE OVERLOOKED

Sometimes an offense is so hurtful, however, that

overlooking it is impossible. You can tell when the line is crossed by one simple test. If you can't get the offense off your mind, it requires going to the offender. Jesus said, "If your brother sins against you,[3] go and tell him his fault between you and him alone. If he hears you, you have gained your brother" (Matthew 18:15).

Offenses of this sort must be dealt with quickly: "'Be angry, and do not sin': do not let the sun go down on your wrath, nor give place to the devil" (Ephesians 4:26–27). God does not intend Christians to stew in their anger; doing so lets Satan get a grip on us. We are instructed to handle each day's offenses on the day they occur. By overlooking offenses where possible and engaging in private rebukes otherwise, most offenses can be laid to rest.

WHAT TO DO WHEN OTHERS ASK FOR YOUR FORGIVENESS

All of us would rather grant forgiveness than request it. Still, it's difficult to forgive someone; if you have never found it difficult to forgive, you have never been adequately offended. A time will almost certainly come when it's hard to grant forgiveness, and God has already given instructions about what to do. The short version is: you always extend forgiveness, and you always extend it upon request. No matter what the offense, no matter how deep your feeling, forgive.

The standard for Christian forgiveness is simple and eloquent: "Be kind to one another, tenderhearted, forgiving one another, just as God in Christ also forgave you" (Ephesians 4:32). If we are glad to be forgiven totally in Christ, we must be equally committed to the principle of forgiving others totally.

Sometimes that can be hard. Corrie ten Boom was arrested by the Germans during World War II for harboring Jews in her home in Haarlem, the Netherlands. Taken to the women's concentration camp at Ravensbruck, she suffered unspeakable horrors that included seeing her sister die in the same camp.

Shortly after the war, Corrie traveled to Germany to share her faith with the people of that devastated nation. Speaking to a group at a church in Munich, extolling the glories of God's forgiveness, she recognized in the crowd the face of one of the Ravensbruck guards. He approached her after the meeting ended, hand outstretched: "A fine message, Fräulein! How good it is to know that, as you say, all our sins are at the bottom of the sea!"

She reflected:

> And I, who had spoken so glibly of forgiveness, fumbled in my pocketbook rather than take that hand. He would not remember me, of course—how could he remember one prisoner among those thousands of women?
>
> But I remembered him and the leather crop swinging from his belt. I was face-to-face with one of my captors and my blood seemed to freeze.
>
> "You mentioned Ravensbruck in your talk," he was saying. "I was a guard there." No, he did not remember me.
>
> "But since that time," he went on, "I have become a Christian. I know that God has forgiven me for the cruel things I did there, but I would like to hear it from your lips as well. Fräulein"—again the hand came out—"will you forgive me?"[4]

At a moment like that, you discover whether forgiveness is a personal commitment or just a word in the dictionary. In Corrie's case, God's grace was sufficient. She did forgive her former tormentor, extending to him the same freeing forgiveness that she had received from God.

WHAT IT MEANS TO FULLY FORGIVE

Because forgiving someone can be so emotionally charged, people often wrestle with the mechanics of it. When they have been deeply wounded, they wonder whether extending forgiveness does not too cheaply dismiss the pain of an episode that may have been life-changing for them.

Forgiveness is not easy to do, but it is simple to define. When someone requests forgiveness, God's Word requires that I extend it. That means making, in effect, a series of three promises to that person. First, *I promise not to raise the offense again as an issue between myself and the offender.* If the offense recurs, and the person requests forgiveness again, I must treat it as though the matter has happened only once. I must not say, "I can't forgive you for this; you offended me once before just this way." I must refuse to allow the forgiven matter to become an issue between us ever again.

This point is particularly important inside a marriage. Mates often have troubles fulfilling the first promise, since they accumulate, through the years, lots of opportunities to offend and be offended. As someone has said, mates don't get hysterical, they get historical.

Secondly, *I promise not to discuss the issue with others,* allowing people outside the offense to become a part of it by initiating their own grudge against the offender. I keep it a private issue as well as a dead issue.

Third, *I promise not to dwell on the offense in my own mind.* I don't promise that I will never think about it (something over which I have no control). I do promise that when it pops into my head I will intentionally occupy my mind with something constructive rather than dwelling on my pain or the offender's misbehavior.

Those are three promises that I—and you—can keep. They don't require superhuman effort, only a commitment to Jesus Christ to handle offenses His way. Keeping those promises will keep lines of communication open. They are a means of treating people as we would like to be treated.

DOES FORGIVING MEAN FORGETTING?

Some say, "I can forgive, but I can never forget what he did." Does forgiving mean forgetting? If by "forgetting" we mean "removing all traces of the offense from the memory," forgiving does not mean forgetting. The offense may intermittently occur to us over a long period —indefinitely, in fact.

I think I hear someone saying, "Ah, but doesn't God say somewhere that He will remember our lawless deeds no more? Aren't we supposed to forgive as He does?" Yes, but we must understand what He means by that. When God promises as part of the new covenant, "I will forgive their iniquity, and their sin I will remember no more" (Jeremiah 31:34), He doesn't mean that the fact of our sin has vanished from His memory. If it did, there would be facts missing from His knowledge. He would no longer be all-knowing, and thus would cease to be God. What He is doing in Jeremiah 31:34 is making the first promise of forgiveness explicit: He will never raise our offenses as an issue between Himself and us again. That is all the forgetting you and I will ever need.

However, when sins are laid to rest biblically, they become less and less of a problem as time passes. You cannot keep from feeling a twinge of pain when the memory of an offense (even a forgiven one) pops unbidden into your mind. You can, however, by keeping the promises of forgiveness, prevent the twinge from becoming an ache.

ABOUT HOLDING A GRUDGE

The alternative to forgiving is holding a grudge, a process that some people manage to turn into an art form. After the Civil War, Robert E. Lee visited a Kentucky woman who took him to the remains of a majestic old oak in front of her home. She bitterly pointed out how its limbs and trunk had been destroyed by Union artillery fire. The woman waited for Lee to burst into similar invective against the North or at least sympathize with her loss, but he said nothing for a while. Finally, he looked at her and said, "Cut it down, my dear madam, and then forget it."[5]

Many a person goes through life with a fixation on the offenses (real or imagined) he has suffered. If nothing particularly interesting is happening at the moment, he likes to play with his grudge. He pulls it out, fondles it, puts it through its paces, pats it on its head, and folds it away lovingly until it is needed again—scarcely realizing that he has been toying with a spiritual cobra. Scientific studies show that bitterness and stress lead to an assortment of physical ailments, which often wound the spirit as well.

S. I. McMillen, a medical doctor, tells the story of a college student named Pierre who consulted him for treatment of a serious stomach problem. Pierre's discomfort, however, refused to respond to medical methods. McMillen, acutely aware of the physical ramifications of unresolved hostility, questioned Pierre about his personal relationships, but the young man denied holding in any resentments.

After the visit, one of Pierre's fellow students told Dr. McMillen how Pierre had recently expressed publicly a hateful distaste for several enemies whom he felt had wronged him years before. The doctor questioned Pierre upon his next visit about these issues, but he again denied there were any such resentments. McMillen concluded that Pierre's grudge was ruling his life: "Paying the price with wretched days and sleepless nights, he fattened his grudges by repeated rehearsals to every available auditor. His only concern was to learn the name of the student who had given me the information. He actually pleaded with me for that name because he wanted to give the boy a tongue lashing." Ultimately, Pierre's health kept him from returning to college.[6]

I have on a number of occasions been involved in pre-funeral briefings which went something like this: "Pastor, you need to understand before you do this funeral that my Uncle Bill and Aunt Sally are here under duress. They only came because they know that the rest of the family will speak ill of them if they didn't come."

"But why would they not come to his brother's funeral?"

"Well, it goes back to 1970, when their father died. He left an old will which specified that his wood-shop tools were to go to Uncle Bill, but Bill's brother insisted that their dad had promised them to him. They haven't spoken to each other in years as a result."

Change the year to a different one and the wood-shop tools to a china cabinet or something else, and the description could apply to hundreds of families. After a while, the ugly demon of pride raises its head, people dig in their heels, and families are fractured—sometimes permanently.

God, however, never made us to hold grudges. We simply aren't equipped to handle the stress. Grudges torture their owners, while the object of the grudge often has no idea that anything is being held against him.

We suffer if we don't forgive. The disciples struggled with this truth when they heard it so often from the Lord Jesus. Peter once approached Him and asked, "Lord, how often shall my brother sin against me, and I forgive him? Up to seven times?" (Matthew 18:21). Peter may have thought that his suggestion was heroic until Jesus brought him up short: "I do not say to you, up to seven times, but up to seventy times seven" (Matthew 18:22); in other words, "As often as he asks."

The Lord then explained the principle by telling a story about a king who wanted to settle accounts with some of his servants. One owed the king a huge fortune and was unable to repay. The king ordered that the debtor and his family be sold into slavery to settle the debt. However, when the offender pleaded with the king for more time, his majesty went even further than he was asked. He forgave the debt entirely. Then the forgiven debtor, forgetting the kindness he had just experienced, went out and treated his own debtors unmercifully.

When news of this reached the palace, the king "was angry, and delivered [the original debtor] to the torturers until he should pay all that was due to him" (Matthew 18:34).

Many have read this account and wondered about the torturers. The Lord by this phrase refers neither to some imaginary purgatory nor to a loss of salvation. The "torturers" live inside the unforgiving person. At the moment you refuse to grant forgiveness to another person, you become locked in an internal struggle about the matter.

"Torturers" is a word that refers to the inner discomfort that the Lord puts into the life of any person who is bitter toward another. Unforgiving people find that they have difficulty sleeping, and they think about the soured relationship during many of their waking moments as well. It isn't what you eat, it's what eats you that really is hard to swallow.

Holding a grudge also inhibits our present relationship with God. After the Lord gave what is commonly called the Lord's Prayer, with its appeal for forgiveness, He included a proviso: "If you forgive men their trespasses, your heavenly Father will also forgive you. But if you do not forgive men their trespasses, neither will your Father forgive your trespasses" (Matthew 6:14–15). His statement does not refer to eternal forgiveness, but to what happens right now. Our present relationship with God is marred when we behave unmercifully toward others.

We of all people need to exhibit a willingness to deal tenderly with the sins against us. God did not build us to live with unresolved hostility, and He even refuses to permit us to have unimpeded fellowship with Him when we try it. The moment we determine to hold a grudge, we also find ourselves in a strained relationship with God.

Nothing can be worth that. And nothing can be better than a restored relationship with people and with God.

NOTES

1. "C. C. McCabe on Forgiveness," Jon Allen, ed., *Illustration Digest,* July–August 1989, 3.
2. *Bits & Pieces,* 15 October 1992, 13.
3. A minority of manuscripts here omit "against you," but even without these words the Lord's intent is clear. Matthew 18:15 does not constitute authorization to become moral policeman to the world.
4. Jack Canfield, Mark Victor Hansen, Patty Aubery, and Patty Mitchell, *Chicken Soup for the Christian Soul* (Deerfield Beach, Fla.: Health Communications, 1997), 2–3. The complete story of Corrie's remarkable experience in World War II, including her forgiving of this tormentor, is found in Corrie ten Boom, *The Hiding Place* (Old Tappan, N.J., Spire, 1971).
5. Charles Bracelen Flood, *Lee: The Last Years,* quoted in James S. Hewett, ed., *Illustrations Unlimited* (Wheaton, Ill.: Tyndale, 1988), 222.
6. S. I. McMillen, *None of These Diseases* (Old Tappan, N. J.: Revell, 1963), 70–71.

Chapter Eleven

THE GOLDEN RULE

AND THE GOSPEL

*T*he phone rang early one morning. A church member, whom I'll call Alvin, was calling. I could tell by the tone of Alvin's voice that he was deeply troubled. "I'm sorry to call, pastor, but one of my employees was arrested last night. It was, well, a morals charge. The guy is facing jail time."

As Alvin explained, the other consequences became clear, including humiliation before his wife and family and, since the charge was connected with his work, the likelihood of being fired.

"I hate to do that," Alvin explained. "He's always been a good employee. I know this is fundamentally a spiritual problem; before I do anything, would you be willing to talk to him? If he can get his life straightened out, I'll postpone a decision about his job until later."

I agreed to meet with "Fred," and Alvin brought him by my office later that day.

It didn't take long to see that Fred was a broken man.

"I'm caught in the grip of a loathsome habit, and I know it," he admitted. "I need help." He wanted to break loose from his problem and head in a new direction; he just didn't know how. Like a lot of people, he had only a superficial understanding of the Christian faith. To him, Christianity was following a list of rules and trying to do your best. He had already tried that, and it hadn't worked.

As we talked and I explained how Christ had come not to reward good intentions but to offer Himself as a sacrifice for sin, the Holy Spirit opened his eyes. "Do you mean that Jesus can forgive even a man like me?" he asked. I affirmed that the Lord could not only forgive but give him the strength to turn away from temptation by planting His own life within.

With tears in his eyes, Fred bowed his head and received Christ as his Savior. Afterward, he expressed a desire to know more about the Lord Jesus. For several weeks we met and went through some of the basics of Christian living and how it related to his current challenges.

Fred was able to keep his job, settle his legal problems, and repair his relationship with his family. He became an active member of a local church. The last time I saw him, the smile on his face looked a yard wide.

FULFILLING THE GOLDEN RULE BY OFFERING OTHERS TRANSFORMED LIVES

The key player in Fred's life wasn't me, of course; it was his boss. Had Alvin not established a good relationship with Fred, the latter would not have been open to consulting Alvin's pastor—or anybody else. Alvin didn't feel competent to deal with Fred's spiritual problem, but he cared enough about him to get him to somebody who could. Alvin's merciful attitude blew away the fog so that Fred could see the reality of the gospel.

Sharing the gospel of Jesus Christ with others is perhaps the most glorious expression of the Golden Rule. No greater act of love can be expressed to others than that of getting God's good news to them. Yet most Christians—I have read estimates as high as 95 percent—never have a part in bringing anyone to Christ. That kind of statistic demands an explanation.

REASONS CHRISTIANS DON'T SHARE THE GOSPEL

Christians don't share the love of Christ with unbelievers for several reasons. At the risk of oversimplifying, four of them seem to stand out in the present cultural climate.

1. *They have no unbelieving friends.* Today, the primary reason we don't share the gospel with people isn't theological but social. Most Christians don't know any unbelievers well enough to interact with them on a spiritual level. The uncomfortable truth is that most people who become drawn to Christ are first drawn to Christians. An even more uncomfortable fact: The longer a person is a Christian, the fewer non-Christians he can number among his friends. He may know a great many, but his relationships are mostly of the superficial variety; not close enough to earn the right to ask personal questions.

2. *They don't understand the stakes.* Another reason why Christians don't share the gospel is theologi-

cal. Deep down, they don't think that Christ is the only solution to man's desperate situation. Without necessarily verbalizing it, they sometimes suspect that God must have an alternate set of methods for allowing decent, respectable people to gain eternal life. What these methods might be, they are at a loss to say; but that doesn't keep them from suspecting that there are some.

3. *They don't know how to verbalize the message.* A third reason why Christians don't share the love of Christ is a practical one. They don't know how to express the gospel correctly; and rather than take a chance on leading someone astray, they simply say little or nothing. This is really more of an excuse than a reason, since that kind of information isn't hard to come by (to say nothing of the simplicity of handing someone a well-written tract or book); but a poor excuse is sometimes better than none at all.

4. *They aren't willing to risk a friendship.* Another cause for the silence of Christians is their reluctance to risk a friendship for the sake of the gospel. They fear that their unbelieving friend will be offended and terminate the relationship.

Of the four reasons, the final one is the least defensible. For one thing, the risk is minimal in most cases. Even a person who isn't interested in the gospel (at the moment) is unlikely to be angry at someone who cares enough to inquire about his soul. Even in the unusual event that a non-Christian terminates the relationship, the Christian has planted an important seed in the unbeliever's heart. Should God bring him to repentance, he now knows at least one person who loves him enough to deal with him on a spiritual level.

Then again, should a Christian—even from his own point of view—be satisfied with a relationship that ignores the spiritual dimension in his life? Any friend doesn't know me well at all if he doesn't understand that Jesus Christ is the most important person in my life. How can I keep that area of my life closed off to him?

HOW YOU CAN SHARE YOUR FAITH

Not every Christian is gifted as an evangelist, but all of us can express His love toward others. We can be part of His plan in bringing people to Christ, treating them as we wanted to be treated—as people who need to find the way to God and hope for the future. Joe Aldrich, author of *Life-Style Evangelism* (Multnomah), one of the best books on the subject, divides sharing the love of Christ into three processes: presence, proclamation, and persuasion. The first provides the context for the gospel; the second, its content; and the third, its application. Not everyone is comfortable taking part in all three expressions of Christ's love, but everybody can be involved in the first two.

PRESENCE

Being part of the life of someone who needs to know Christ is the first and most critical step in sharing His love. Loving another for Christ's sake and being a genuine friend helps us earn the right to engage in personal conversations. You may be the only genuine Christian in the other person's life; it is important that he knows that you are his friend whether or not he is interested in your faith.

Today, he may not be. Tomorrow, things may change. A woman in my church, who I will call Jackie, told a neighbor about the gospel. But Jackie found that Karen was not open to spiritual things. Still Jackie remained Karen's friend; in their ongoing friendship, Jackie showed respect by not forcing Karen into conversations about spiritual matters. Then one day Karen came home to discover that her husband had committed suicide. Once past the shock, she needed answers, and the only person she knew to ask was Jackie, the friend who had shown an interest in the spiritual side of her life. In time, she came to receive Christ; but things might have been different if the only Christian she knew well had offended her by twisting her spiritual arm. Such tactics, among other things, show a complete disregard for the ability of God to move in the person's life in ways that may be unseen.

And He is working; make no mistake. He is always involved with people who don't know Him, though the work may be invisible to an outsider. He continues to chip away at people's hard hearts because He loves them more than we do, but it helps to have someone near them whose love for Christ is authentic.

Being a loving presence for Christ's sake is a beginning; but at some point, the content of the gospel will need to be shared.

PROCLAMATION

We proclaim the love of God when we share the content of the gospel with someone who hasn't yet believed it. In *Loving God,* Charles Colson described

Boris Kornfeld, a Jewish doctor sentenced to a Siberian prison camp during Stalin's Russia. Dr. Kornfeld met a Christian believer (whose name is unknown) in the camp. He apparently was a man of authentic faith, whose sincerity and frequent reciting of the Lord's Prayer made an impression on Kornfeld.

The horrors of camp life, many of which were inflicted by brutal guards, took their toll on Boris Kornfeld's soul. Once, when repairing a guard's artery that had been damaged in a knifing, the doctor, going against all of his training and oaths, found himself thinking what a pleasure it would be to leave a strategic suture loose. One poorly tied knot, and a brutal guard would quietly bleed to death. As he paused over the wound, he caught himself. Horrified with the hostility that he had discovered residing in his own heart, he found himself repeating the phrase from the Lord's Prayer that he had heard from his Christian friend: "Forgive us our sins, as we forgive those who sin against us."

Soon afterward, Kornfeld began refusing to overlook some of the typical vices of the camp. Eventually he turned in an orderly who had stolen food from a dying patient. In doing so, he knew he had signed his own death warrant. The orderly (or one of his friends) would soon come after him.

One afternoon, Dr. Kornfeld examined a surgical patient who had been recently operated on for cancer and whose face reflected enormous misery. The physician shared his experience in detail with the patient, who became, through the doctor's testimony, a Christian himself. True to his expectations, Dr. Kornfeld was murdered that very night; but his testimony (and the horrors of the gulag) lived on through the writings of his patient, Aleksandr Solzhenitsyn.[1]

You can proclaim the gospel conversationally, just as Kornfeld told Solzhenitsyn. If you don't know how to get into it gracefully, there are lots of resources available that will provide direction. James Kennedy's *Evangelism Explosion* (Tyndale) contains a complete evangelistic conversation. The late Paul Little's *How to Give Away Your Faith* (InterVarsity) covers many of the essentials. Win and Charles Arn's *The Master's Plan for Making Disciples* (Baker) talks about how to share the love of Christ through the natural relationships of neighborhood and work. Bob and Betty Jacks' *Your Home a Lighthouse* (NavPress) describes ways to proclaim the truth of God's love while extending hospitality. Your Christian bookseller can suggest others.

If you are still unsure of yourself after reading some of those resources, think about letting a good book do your proclamation, and don't overlook the most obvious one: the Bible. Inexpensive Bibles and Scripture portions are easy to come by nowadays. Ask a friend if he has ever read the gospel of John. Hand him a Bible or gospel in a fairly recent translation and suggest that he read it and share with you his impressions. Let the Spirit of God use His Word to accomplish His ends.

I once studied under a man named George Peters who discovered the power of the Word for himself. George was born in Russia just before the Bolshevik Revolution. His family did not sympathize with the communists, and George saw his father dragged off to prison. Later a communist shot George's uncle through the head in his presence. The rest of the family decided that it was just a matter of time before they suffered a similar fate. They left Russia discreetly and began traveling through Europe, looking for a country that would take them in; but nobody wanted them. They wandered, looking for political asylum, couldn't find it, and sailed for the Americas.

Eventually, the family was allowed to enter Mexico. But their experience had left them bitter and hateful people. The Peterses were caught in the grip of hostility against the world.

While they were living in Mexico, someone sent the family a package. They never did discover where it came from. Opening it, the Peterses discovered a Bible, an English translation. Their English was only fair, and the family decided that they would throw it away. But one thing stopped them. The Bible was obviously very expensive. It had gilt-edged paper and a leather binding; someone had spent some serious money on it. So they decided to try to read it.

"For some reason, I decided to begin reading at the book of Revelation," George later told me. Imagine the scene: a Russian teenager, living in Mexico, reading an English Bible in the book of Revelation. Even though humanly speaking that is a recipe for failure, the Word of God spoke to this young man's heart and he read on. In fact, he became a Christian believer while reading.

As he expanded his exploration of the Scriptures, he felt his old hostility and bitterness melting away. Peters determined to give his life to Christ in dedicated ministry. Eventually he moved to Canada for theological training. He became Dr. Peters and spent much of his career as a professor of missions at Dallas Theological Seminary.

Beyond your proclamation by giving a book, consider other resources; for instance, offer an audiotape. It may be a gifted speaker or simply the powerful Word of God on tape. That's what happened to Eddie, someone I heard about through my friend Stan Howard.

The two men saw each other at a funeral, and Stan was amazed at the change in Eddie. When Stan had last seen him, Eddie often went without a shirt. He wasn't making a fashion statement; Eddie simply knew that any given shirt was likely to be ripped from his body at any time in a fistfight. Eddie lost an eye in 1971 in one encounter with a motorcycle gang.

Years later, Eddie had married and become a partner in a service company, but he still was in and out of trouble. His arrest record grew longer. One evening, after winning a tidy sum shooting pool, Eddie sat down to rest for a minute when his opponent, high on cocaine, clubbed him with a pool cue. The blow fractured his jaw and upper palate and destroyed his remaining eye.

While Eddie lay in the hospital thinking of ways to get even, a friend dropped by and left him a gift: the New Testament on audiocassette. Eddie couldn't easily ignore the gesture, since the man who left the tapes was once himself a man of Eddie's stripe, but who was now obviously living a different sort of life.

As Stan explained in his letter, "Eddie was finally sent home, but he returned as a new man in Christ. Eddie dropped the attempted murder charges against his assailant, though federal authorities prosecuted anyway." The prosecuting attorney and presiding judge couldn't understand why Eddie wanted to drop charges on a man who tried to kill him.

Eddie replied, "I now have love in my heart; the hate is gone. I guess I had to become blind so that I could see."

God can use the kindness of a hospital visit coupled with some well-chosen tapes to effect spiritual change in a person's heart. The presence of a credible friend supplies the music of the gospel; the proclamation of the tapes provides the words.

PERSUASION

Handing someone a book or a set of tapes may be all that is needed, but for some people more is required. Persuasion can be and often is part of making the love of Christ personal to others. When Paul came to Ephesus, the book of Acts says that "he went into the synagogue and spoke boldly for three months, reasoning and *persuading* concerning the things of the kingdom of God" (Acts 19:8, italics added). Later, when Paul arrived in Rome, the same writer explained, "Many came to him at his lodging, to whom he explained and solemnly testified of the kingdom of God, *persuading* them concerning Jesus from both the Law of Moses and the Prophets" (Acts 28:23).

When many Christians think of sharing the gospel of Christ, persuasion is what they think of. Yet it is the last link in the chain for most people. In fact, not everybody needs persuading, a word which suggests the presence of resistance. When Peter was called to Caesarea to share the truth of God's love with Cornelius, a Roman centurion, he was unable even to finish his oration before Cornelius and his family believed: "While Peter was still speaking these words, the Holy Spirit fell upon all those who heard the word" (Acts 10:44). God had done the preparing; all that was necessary was proclamation.

Still, many people are reluctant to accept the gift of life offered in the gospel. They have questions and points of resistance. Respect for them as persons—loving them as ourselves—dictates that we take these matters seriously. It is possible, to be sure, that they are simply blowing smoke in our faces. Their questions may simply be distractions or excuses; but if they are, that will be apparent in time. We don't persuade by cynically assuming that our non-Christian friends are lying to us. We do what the Golden Rule says we must do. We give them the same kind of respect we would want if we were sitting where they are.

As you seek to obey the Golden Rule, ask God to open doors of conversation so that you can share what Jesus Christ has done for you. You may find that the greatest joy in Christian living is helping others find Christ.

NOTES

1. Charles W. Colson, *Loving God* (Grand Rapids: Zondervan, 1983), 27–34.

Chapter Twelve

WHERE DO I DRAW THE LINE?

*E*very Christian who takes the Golden Rule seriously has been torn, at one time or another, by an inner conflict. It's unavoidable. If you seek to give yourself fully and regularly to others, a conflict arises, produced by two facts:

1. People all around me have needs, some of them very great.
2. My resources to meet those needs are limited.

Nothing I can write is likely to erase that conflict entirely, but a book on the Golden Rule ought to contain at least a few guidelines for helping people deal with the tension.

How you practice the Golden Rule in your life should revolve around a plan, a plan that reflects priorities based on biblical principles, your spiritual gifts, and the most effective use of your time. In all your decisions to implement the Golden Rule, of course, the ultimate goal is to honor Christ. Here are three guidelines for doing so.

DEVELOP A PERSONAL STRATEGY

Many people decide on how they will obey the Golden Rule largely on the basis of impulse. Someone calls on them to engage in a ministry or respond to a need, and they either refuse or comply according to their on-the-fly evaluation of the requests brought to them. A better approach is to think through an overarching strategy for your life and take the initiative to engage in ministries based on your gifts, abilities, and interests.

Take some time to ask yourself questions like:

- Where can I be most effective for the cause of Christ?
- What is my spiritual gift?
- What needs exist around me that I could be instrumental in meeting?
- Do I have a burden for a particular area of ministry that no one else seems to be addressing?
- When I stand before the judgment seat of Christ, what area of my life will I be most proud of? What area will cause me the most embarrassment?
- What is my mission in life? Do I know it well enough to write it out in a couple of brief sentences?

Until you can supply answers to these questions, you may not be ready to say "no" to anything. That makes you a candidate for joining the ranks of the compulsively busy—to overdo, overgive, and overspend your resources. Many people address the issue of their limitations by pretending they don't have any; but all of us do. Every thoughtful Christian knows that if he ignores his boundaries he will in time become a depleted person, with little ability to help anyone.

FOLLOW SCRIPTURAL PRINCIPLES

Make decisions on who, when, and how to help by following scriptural principles. The most obvious (though not necessarily the most profound) kinds of questions needing the biblical perspective concern financial issues. Does the Golden Rule oblige me to give money to every panhandler I run across? Or is it unchristian to simply provide funds? Shouldn't I take the man who is asking for money for food to a restaurant to make sure he doesn't take my contribution to the nearest liquor store?

Scripture does recognize the legitimacy of giving according to one's ability. Paul urged the Corinthians to be liberal in their giving to the poor saints of Judea, using the Macedonian Christians as an example: "For I bear witness that according to their ability, yes, and beyond their ability, they were freely willing, imploring us with much urgency that we would receive the gift and the fellowship of the ministering to the saints" (2 Corinthians 8:3–4). Paul does not mean that the Macedonians possessed $100,000 but gave $150,000 away. Rather, the Macedonians gave even more than should have been expected of them, based on their income. Their abilities were modest, but they gave liberally. They were happy to do so; but before they gave, Paul had an idea of what might reasonably be expected from them.

It helps little, in addressing this issue of our limitations, to piously appeal to the riches of heaven, as in "Yes, you're limited; but you have forgotten all the wealth of your heavenly Father. He can provide what you lack. You need to exercise faith."

Yes, God does have abilities greater than my own. Yes, I do need to exercise faith. However, when a man is standing before you with his hand out, you don't have the ability to call a prayer meeting and ask God to send funds. When the phone rings, you have to decide *now* what to do.

Not only that, there is a vast difference between knowing God's abilities and knowing His intentions at this moment. We have no reason to believe that money will materialize in our wallets as we walk down the street. And if it did, where would be the joy that comes from giving sacrificially from limited resources?

Asking "What Would Jesus Do?"

Nor is there much help in asking the question, "What would Jesus do?" (No, the answer is not, "Sell your WWJD bracelets, watches, pens, bicycles, radios, tennis shoes, and microwaves and give the proceeds to the poor.") While I am always sympathetic to anyone thinking of ways to please God, this question has its limits in helping any person do that.

The answer to the question, "What would Jesus do?" is, "Probably the last thing you would expect." We have a large ability to kid ourselves about how confidently we can predict what He would do in a given instance. We are on sounder ground to know and observe a few key principles of Scripture related to giving our time and our finances.

THE PRINCIPLE OF DIVINE ORIGIN

One critical factor, often overlooked, is what might be called the principle of love's divine origin. The impulse to love others comes from God, not from the existence of people's needs. We love because He first loved us. While needy people sometimes attempt to manipulate by questioning the godliness of people who don't give generously to them, such attempts to exploit are rarely valid.

However, Jesus Christ has every right to call your choices into question. He asks us to search our hearts, to explore our motives. (See Jesus' warning about our heart's intent in the Sermon on the Mount, especially Matthew 6:1–6, 19–21.) The person who is asking for help probably doesn't know our motive (though that may not keep him from trying to guess and even manipulate us). On the other hand, thoughtless giving can even be an expression of selfishness—looking for a warm feeling instead of expressing the Golden Rule.

THE PRINCIPLE OF PRIORITY

A second factor is the principle of priority. When the need is for life itself, other principles fade into the background. The man who fell among thieves in the parable of the Good Samaritan was nearly dead. Life takes priority over routine questions of charity. If you are close by and can save a life, save it. Less pressing matters have to be evaluated according to other biblical principles.

This principle has been practiced on the world's battlefields throughout the twentieth century. Medics and nurses engaged in triage, sorting patients and allocate limited supplies and time in treating battle victims. It's a system that prioritizes in order to maximize the number of survivors. Triage looks at the most severely wounded, those with the most urgent needs, and tries to help them first, unless such assistance has little likelihood of making a difference. In a sense, we may need to practice a kind of triage when our time and resources are limited. In prayer, we should consult with the Master Physician, seeking wisdom in finding the most needy, the most receptive to physical and spiritual assistance.

THE PRINCIPLE OF PROVIDENCE

Another factor is the principle of God's providence. God places every believer at the center of concentric circles of friends and acquaintances. No one else knows your circumstances, neighborhood, and community as you do. If you don't get behind the ministries of your own local church and ministries to your own community, people on the outside certainly won't. If you can't, in good conscience, support the ministries and missionaries of your church, go to a church where you can.

You may be the only Christian some of your friends know. God has given you those friends. If you do not express the love of Christ to them, who will?

THE PRINCIPLE OF FAMILY PRIORITY

Paul told the Galatian believers that when it comes to charity, members of God's family come first: "Therefore, as we have opportunity, let us do good to all, especially to those who are of the household of faith" (Galatians 6:10). We must share our resources not only with other believers, but when believers are in need, we should take pains to see that their needs are addressed first.

Those outside the faith will sometimes resent this priority, of course. However, providing for the needs of believers first not only helps them, it bears testimony to the reality of Christ. By loving Christians, we show the world that we are Christ's disciples (see John 13:35).

THE PRINCIPLE OF PERSONAL RESPONSIBILITY

In the church at Thessalonica, an assembly with a serious expectation of the second coming of Christ, some believers decided to stop working (probably in view of what they felt was the imminence of that event). As a result, they were living on the kindness and generosity of others in the church.

When Paul heard about the situation, he wrote the church and reminded them, "When we were with you, we commanded you this: If anyone will not work, neither shall he eat" (2 Thessalonians 3:10). He thus established the principle that it is valid to ask whether the recipients of charity—even Christian recipients—are doing all they can to care for themselves before extending charitable ministry to them.

In deciding upon a strategy of engagement, biblical wisdom also suggests that we remember personal obligations that have to be met in addition to our ministry to others. For example, it would be hard to justify depriving my children of essentials in order to minister in the community. (On the other hand, it is important that they not only see me minister to others, but develop the habit themselves.) It would also be presumptuous—unloving, in fact—of me to commit myself to a ministry that demands sacrifices on the part of my wife without asking for her consent.

THE PRINCIPLE OF WELFARE

The principle of welfare asks, "Will I truly be helping a street person if I give him cash?" In some cases, the answer will be "Absolutely." In other situations, the answer will be less obvious. The fact that answering this question may leave us with money in our pocket doesn't mean that it shouldn't be asked. When it comes to offering financial help, sometimes the best help is to refrain from reaching into our wallets. There may be other things we can do to help instead.

On occasion, the loving action by us may be no action at all. Marvin Olasky described several social experiments in which recipients of charity held coupons entitling them to free meals and/or lodging; they also were encouraged to become more independent. In one of the experiments, during a five-year period more than 90,000 tickets were distributed by a Denver shelter offering a free meal and the possibility of a job; only twenty-four were returned. Of those, no one went to the next step and accepted a job.[1]

The first question that the Golden Rule poses is, "Am I helping the other person?" Regrettably, much of the time we won't know the answer to this one.

ADDRESS URGENT NEEDS FIRST

Paul instructed Titus, "Send Zenas the lawyer and Apollos on their journey with haste, that they may lack nothing. And let our people also learn to maintain good works, to meet urgent needs, that they may not be unfruitful" (Titus 3:13–14). Help missionaries like Zenas and Apollos get where they're going, he said, and help them generously, so that they don't have to pinch drachmas; and, in general, try to solve pressing problems where you can. The statement itself presupposes that some needs—less urgent ones—will have to wait.

Earlier we mentioned the concept of *triage,* meeting the most vital needs first. Doing so is not foolproof; we do make errors in assessing needs. Even if you apply the principles I just mentioned, you will likely make mistakes in sharing your resources—on both ends of the spectrum. You will probably leave some valid needs unmet, and you will likely provide assistance to those who don't really need it. When those things happen, it is tempting to call for a pox on the whole business and withdraw.

Just because you cannot solve every problem, however, doesn't mean that you should not be involved in solving any of them. The one who said "You have the poor with you always" (Matthew 26:11) is also the one who has done more for the poor than anyone ever has. Still, when He ascended to the Father He left many poor people behind who had never been directly touched by Him. He also left many beyond reach of the gospel, others in physical or emotional pain, and still others who needed to be discipled. But He made a difference in those whose lives He touched.

And with His help, so can we.

NOTE

1. Marvin Olasky, "Got Some Spare Change?" *World,* 27 April 1996, 30. Available on the Internet at www.worldmag.com/world/issue/04-27-96/closing_2.asp.

EPILOGUE

*O*bedience to the Golden Rule produces the most positive lifestyle imaginable. As we have seen, in loving our enemies, we can transform them. In praying for others, we change ourselves as well as call upon God's assistance. In presenting the good news of Christ's act of salvation, we can transform others, restoring their relationship with God.

But what about the previous, final chapter? When we talked about "drawing the line," we implied hardship and noted drawing limits in our service. Yes, it's true, there are limits. And we need wisdom when it comes to knowing our boundaries. Yet more risks exist for those who neglect the Golden Rule than for those who overdo it. As Christian soldiers, we are called to serve, and the Golden Rule is one vital part of our marching orders.

The Second Great Commandment (see Matthew 22:37–39) can either enlarge us or diminish us according to how we respond to it. If you take the Golden Rule seriously, your life and your outlook will be broadened and enriched—to say nothing of those whom you love as yourself. Short of the second coming of Christ, attention to the Golden Rule is the best hope this world has going for it. In a real sense, our lives depend on it.

As we consider the outcome of obeying the Golden Rule, recognize that the risks will remain. Yet whenever we obey God's commands, His rewards, over time, will follow. When you practice loving others—including the unlovely—you honor God. And those who honor God will be honored by God (see 1 Samuel 2:30).

Be creative and regular in following the Golden Rule. During 1997, *Christianity Today* ran a series of five articles describing what the church is doing right as the millennium draws to a close. The one hundred items mentioned in the series constitute a representative sampling of what can be done when Christians determine to follow the dictates of the Master and love their neighbors as themselves.

Here are a few of the items:

- Not long ago, a group of teens and adults in Montgomery, Alabama, spent their free time by trimming the vegetation around thirty-three homes (mostly of elderly or disabled people). Their purpose was not only to improve the appearance of the yards, but also to remove places that could conceal burglars or vandals.
- The Police Chaplain Corps of Minneapolis is a group of ordained clergy who volunteer free time to assist law enforcement personnel. They help the authorities in sensitive matters like notifying peo-

ple when a member of the family has died, in helping survivors when someone commits suicide, and
in domestic disputes.

• Each year in Oklahoma City a group of Christians
and concerned citizens solicits donations of wheel-
chairs, walkers, and crutches for use by people with
health problems. In a five-year period, they collected more than $250,000 worth of equipment. The
items are redistributed all over the world by Joni
And Friends Ministries.

• One group of believers in Charlotte, North Carolina, keeps a list of trained volunteers who have survived such traumas as cancer, anorexia, incest, and
rape. When people who are dealing with such
upheavals want to talk to someone who understands, the group (which calls itself Kindred Spirits)
matches volunteers with those who are struggling.

• Alan Farley of Appomattox, Virginia, used to take
part in Civil War battle reenactments as a hobby.
Now it is his ministry. He began an organization
that reprints evangelistic tracts from the Civil War
era and distributes them during reenactments.
Because his work replicates the actual ministry of
wartime chaplains, he can even take part in battles
restaged by government agencies. He and his fellow
chaplains have distributed 750,000 tracts and seen
over seven hundred professions of faith in the
process.

• A group of Christians in Bismarck, North Dakota,
seeks out donors to invest in livestock, then finds
ranchers to provide feed and care for the animals
until they are sold. During 1996, $445,000 in profits

from their efforts were distributed among eighty mission organizations.

Few of these ministries ever capture public notice, but heaven is certainly aware of them. A million years from now, the golden difference they made in human lives will be celebrated in the kingdom of God.

Today it is our privilege to be His representatives to this tarnished and troubled world. Let us extend to it the love it so desperately needs in His matchless name.

REVIEW AND STUDY GUIDE

INTRODUCTION

*T*he purpose of the Foundations of the Faith series is to reacquaint the reader with some of the great doctrines and favorite Scripture passages relating to our Christian life. Indeed, these books attempt to link together our faith as we understand it and our life as we live it. Though our goal is to provide more in-depth teaching on a topic, we hope to accomplish this with a popular style and practical application. Books in the series include the Lord's Prayer, the Beatitudes, and Psalm 23.

In keeping with our goal of a popular-level treatment, this review and study guide is not meant to involve exhaustive digging, but to reinforce the important concepts (through "Points to Consider") and to help you explore some of their implications (through "Questions and Response").

A book's impact is judged in the long term, and if you can retain at least one important point per chapter and answer and act upon some of the questions relevant to your life, you have made considerable progress. May God bless your walk with Him as you enter into these exercises.

JAMES S. BELL JR.

Chapter One

1. Religious authorities may have hundreds of rules, but Jesus reduced their validity to two—loving God above all and your neighbor as yourself.

2. The Golden Rule is not a burdensome command, but rather it provides opportunities to be indispensable to others, because our neighbors need us.

3. Today, there are many negative twists on the Golden Rule, many dealing with getting even. Such versions can never provide the satisfaction of giving your neighbor more good than you receive.

4. The good works of various Christian charities, which have blessed multiple generations, are simply their interpretation of living out the Golden Rule. Without these contributions, our society wouldn't be the same.

QUESTIONS AND RESPONSE

1. Review the characteristics of Christian behavior that Aristides describes to the Emperor Hadrian in the second century. Which ones are closely followed by today's Christians and which are not? What impact in general does this have on our society?

2. Encouragement and support for others are major elements of the Golden Rule. How might you put them into practice with someone today?

Chapter Two

POINTS TO CONSIDER

1. Since many people view love as an emotional feeling rather than an act of will, they think the Golden Rule must really be an impossible ideal since we can't feel strongly about everyone.

2. The Golden Rule is not arbitrary or imposed upon us but part of the reality of life—lived in all its richness if we obey it or making us miserable if we do not.

3. Loving others is another form of loving ourselves. It enhances our being and allows us the personal satisfaction of fulfilling God's purposes—for ourselves and others.

4. Love is composed of three distinct forms: attraction (personal worth), natural affection (familial), and willful determination (godly). These may overlap but each supercedes mere emotion.

QUESTIONS AND RESPONSE

1. If love is based on the will, the qualities of 1 Corinthians 13 best typify our necessary responses to others. Rank them in order beginning with the one you do best. How can you improve upon those at the lower end of the scale?

2. When have you found that loving your neighbor gets you into difficulties because it is controversial? When have you avoided a loving response for that very reason?

Chapter Three

1. Our natural inclination is to limit the scope of the Golden Rule, eliminating those people or situations that are seemingly uncomfortable, unjust, or unfair.

2. Being busy, even with good things, doesn't justify our ignoring the "interruptions" of people with needs that may not fit our previous plans.

3. In Christ we have been set free to pray for and do good to our enemies. In this way their offenses do not reduce us, because we choose not to react in kind.

4. Because we have been given many privileges, including education and affluence, we have a responsibility to reach out and share our many resources with those in other parts of the world less fortunate than we.

Questions and Response

1. Look back at the Pennsylvania consulting group's survey on time spent in our lifetime. What time spent in the course of a given month could be redirected to serve those who need our time or assistance?

2. Consider a short-term missions project that will serve others outside your culture. If you are not able to do this in the near future, get involved in supporting a venture, going beyond donating money.

Chapter Four

Points to Consider

1. God's love lifts us up and makes us better people because we're valued by Him. Likewise, we should exalt others to help them reach their full potential.

2. God reaches out and loves us unconditionally because it's a part of His character. When Christ moves into our lives, He'll have us do the same, regardless of how others respond.

3. God doesn't stop loving us even when we resist. We are called to persist in our love for others even when they seem unlovable.

4. God's love frees us from bondage but does not control us. We too can help others let go of their pain and be liberated from their weaknesses.

Questions and Response

1. We are all egocentric and see things from our own perspective. Where and why are you weakest in terms of your relationships? How can you broaden your outlook to include their viewpoint?

2. Entering into someone's pain is uncomfortable and unnatural, yet it is central to the essence of love. Minister to a friend or acquaintance who is suffering today.

Chapter Five

POINTS TO CONSIDER

1. God wants us to find complete satisfaction and pleasure in Him, but when we pursue substitutes we find only boredom and despair.

2. There is a direct correlation between happiness and unselfishness, for when you bless others you yourself receive the greatest satisfaction.

3. God always provides benefits when we keep His commands, though He is not obligated to do so. He wants to motivate and reward us for doing His will.

4. God does not want us to be detached lovers. Though we are commanded to love regardless of feelings, He wants us to build up a holy passion for others that requires our whole being.

QUESTIONS AND RESPONSE

1. Try to recall the time when you were most blessed by serving someone else. What was the nature of the blessing, even if you didn't receive anything tangible in return?

2. Think back to the times when you pursued various things to make yourself happy. Why did they fail to deliver the goods? What does this say about the merits of getting the most out of life to satisfy yourself?

Chapter Six

Points to Consider

1. You may be able to achieve great goals in life, but the ability to maintain self-control in trying circumstances may prove much harder to accomplish.

2. If we fear God, we will not fear man and will be able to take the risks necessary to love others boldly. Loving others biblically means first overcoming our fears of failure.

3. Loving others to the fullest is a high-risk adventure, but our Master promises to remain faithful as we in turn reach out to others in a way that goes beyond our natural capabilities.

4. Anger inside is a normal reaction, especially to unrighteous action; but harsh words go beyond what is called for, wounding others and destroying relationships.

Questions and Response

1. When has your justifiable anger erupted into harsh words that wounded the souls of others? Seek forgiveness from someone you have hurt and pursue a better way of dealing with anger.

2. When has fear of another's response, even from someone who has been favorable toward you, eliminated your chance of doing a good deed? What was the root of your fear?

Chapter Seven

1. We often want recognition of service to others without the difficulties or the work, because we don't realize that the hard path is the best way to the greatest rewards.

2. Though Jesus was acting in complete servanthood at the Cross, He was in control of events, and it was His own decision for the purpose of attaining a higher good.

3. Noble self-sacrifice in a worthy cause can influence more people than we realize and turn the tide away from self-interest to mutual care and concern.

4. Setbacks in life can give you compassion for others in a similar predicament. If you open your heart to others with understanding, your own pain may lessen.

Questions and Response

1. Hospitality is a form of service that almost everyone can render. Begin small by asking someone you don't know well who might be needy to come home for a meal. Then think about doing this on a regular basis.

2. There are a number of forms of service that you may not be gifted at or qualified to do. But there are many others that may be simple and almost easy to overlook. Consider a small step to serving in the latter category.

Chapter Eight

POINTS TO CONSIDER

1. By responding negatively, even when it seems justified, we may lose the opportunity for reconciliation with our enemy at a later time.

2. Our view of ourselves should originate from what God thinks of us and has done for us, rather than from the opinions of others.

3. Kindness and humility are more effective weapons against difficult people than pointing out where they are wrong or trying to punish them for bad behavior.

4. We need to keep our eyes on the priorities that God has for us in the church rather than disputing minor points or allowing a divisive spirit.

QUESTIONS AND RESPONSE

1. Think of those who oppose you or irritate you. Is it due to godliness, neutral behavior, or perhaps partially because there is some weakness in you?

2. Division in the church is a very serious offense toward God. What criteria at times make division necessary, and what other issues imply that we stay together even when it is uncomfortable?

Chapter Nine

1. If we would want others to pray for us, knowing we need divine help, we should be willing to make it a major habit to pray for others, because they need it just as much.

2. As we make a commitment to pray for new people or situations, our interest and attachment grow and we are inclined to have a greater involvement, knowing we are cooperating with God.

3. The more things that we pray about persistently, the more opportunity God has to show us results; which in turn fosters greater confidence in God and His ability to respond to our requests.

4. Offering to pray for others without being asked may require some initial courage. Yet many people truly appreciate the offer and are also then willing to discuss spiritual things.

QUESTIONS AND RESPONSE

1. Make a prayer list of three new people who you know have specific needs. Commit yourself to pray for them every day for the next week and, if possible, tell them of your plan.

2. If prayer sometimes implies greater involvement in someone's life, what can you do beyond praying for someone or some cause that God has put on your heart?

Chapter Ten

1. Conflict is a part of life when it comes to relationships, but because people don't know how to reconcile through forgiveness, they often drift apart in the relationship.

2. Jesus commands that we always take the first step in reconciliation, even if the majority of the fault lies with the other party; otherwise, few relationships would be healed.

3. Though it is sometimes very difficult to forgive excessive offenses, we never have an excuse to withhold forgiveness because of what Jesus did for us as undeserving sinners.

4. Though we may not be able to literally and completely forget a forgiven offense, the very act of genuine forgiveness precludes us from harboring any resentment or bitterness.

QUESTIONS AND RESPONSE

1. Analyze how your lack of forgiveness or harboring of ill feelings after an offense can make you suffer rather than the one who wounded you. How can *you* change this predicament and be set free?

2. Thankfully, God does not want us to live in alienation from Himself or others. Summarize in your own words first how God has made restoration possible and then what steps He requires you to take to make it happen.

Chapter Eleven

1. Christians don't share the gospel because they isolate themselves, don't consider the eternal consequences, can't express the gospel message, or don't want to offend others.

2. There are many ways to present the gospel to others besides verbally. You can share print, audio, or visual resources in a way that still makes it personal.

3. Not everyone needs to be persuaded as we share the gospel of Christ, but if they offer resistance we need to respect both them and their objections.

4. We may not see others converted when we share the gospel partly because we are not present in others' lives; we do not live the message that we proclaim.

QUESTIONS AND RESPONSE

1. What are your greatest strengths and weaknesses when it comes to proclaiming the gospel? When you think of the eternal consequences, what will it take to overcome these deficiencies?

2. Practice the presence of Christ in the life of someone else. Be a servant by asking yourself what Jesus would do for them, and then follow through.

Chapter Twelve

POINTS TO CONSIDER

1. It is important to know ahead of time your guidelines for how and when to help others, because the needs around you are limitless but your resources are not.

2. Though God has unending resources, we don't always know His intentions. Through prayer and discernment, we receive insight and wise strategy for each unique case of need.

3. We can be overwhelmed with the problems of the world. Although we can't solve them all, Jesus left His unfinished work for us to complete His plan for those He wishes to reach.

4. We can be assured that divine providence has placed us in the circle of influence where God wants us to be and our priorities begin with those closest in the family of God.

QUESTIONS AND RESPONSE

1. Review your financial giving over the last year. Based on the principles of this chapter (and the book as a whole), is it sufficient and is it allocated correctly? What changes might you make in the near future?

2. Look also at the areas where you may have crossed the line financially. Where did you give too much, to the wrong people, or for the wrong reasons?

Be sure to read all of the titles in the "Foundations of the Faith" Series:

All You Need to Believe
The Apostles' Creed
C. Donald Cole
3053-8 $8.99

With the vast array of religions and beliefs erupting in the world, how can we be sure of what we believe? How can we defend our beliefs using the Bible, not just from tradition? Read about how the Apostles' Creed presents the truths of the Gospel.

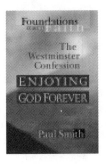

Enjoying God Forever
The Westminster Confession
Paul Smith
7109-9 $9.99

Discover afresh the truth of the Bible and the passionate commitment to it held by the men who authored the Westminster Confession.

On Our Knees and In His Arms
The Lord's Prayer
Peter Lewis
3051-1 $9.99

The Lord's Prayer is an important part of our Christian heritage. More than mere tradition, the prayer is a glimpse into the very Person and purposes of God. Learn why we pray and how the world is changed through prayer.

Song of the Shepherd
Psalm 23
Mark A. Tabb
6190-5 $8.99

If God is to be our Shepherd, we need to be His
sheep. We must surrender our stubborn wills to His
direction, bow to His discipline, and acknowledge
His sovereignty over all heaven and earth. Learn
how to live each day rendered to our Shepherd.

The Only Way to Happiness
The Beatitudes
John F. MacArthur, Jr.
3054-6 $9.99

MacArthur examines Jesus' timeless definition of
happiness, and explains that our reward for following
Jesus' plan is citizenship in the kingdom of God and
an abiding joy that can never be taken away.